Toxic Mayhem

by

Vinson Chard

To my Long Suffering Wife Christine

CHAPTER 1

*D*uring most of the eighties I had been employed as a Process Engineer working in the hi-tech industry with excellent, well-paid jobs. However, once again, life shuffled my particular deck of cards, dealing me a new hand. So here I was in the middle of 1989, out of work and seeking employment. Recently the situation concerning redundancy and unemployment had become just a bit too repetitive for my liking, prompting my morale, confidence and self-esteem to plummet. D*éjà vu* being insufficient a cliché to describe what seemed to be a recurring situation. There appeared no urgency to sign on at the Job Centre, my thoughts being, *'What's the point, there are so few jobs out there?'*

This was becoming ridiculous. I had been made redundant from three jobs in almost twelve months. Thankfully, on the other two occasions, I had managed to find employment within a short period of time. Throughout most of the decade I had somehow managed to escape the ravages and devastating effects of Margaret Thatcher's draconian fiscal policies. Unfortunately, during the period 1988 - 1989 the cards of life dictated I too should now become part of those unemployed statistics, not just once but on three separate occasions, joining the ever-expanding legions of *Maggie's Millions.*

Having divorced my wife Cindy, or to be more precise, Cindy having divorced me, in 1988, I moved back to my home town of Ebbw Vale, where I now lived with Stella, the female catalyst in the steady collapse and ultimate annihilation of my marriage to the attractive Cindy. During the final two years of the

4

eighties, my life appeared to be in complete tumult and disarray, both emotionally and career-wise.

After a period of time, on this, the third occasion of being made redundant, finally relenting, I thought it prudent to sign on at the Job Centre. A fair interval of time had passed since being informed by the official receiver concerning the ruination of the Parrot Corporation, where I had worked for a brief period in the production department (six weeks to be precise). The Parrot Corporation had been a new and relatively short-lived player in the field of manufacturing 3.5 inch floppy discs for the exponentially developing computer world of personal computers. The entire Parrot workforce had been made redundant, not, in all fairness, because of the Tory party, but primarily due to some financially illegal shenanigans perpetrated by the founding Managing Director of the company. Unlawful misappropriation of company funds by the head of the company persuaded the major shareholders, mostly pension funds, to withdraw all of their investments, the proverbial *'rats leaving the sinking ship.'* The corollary being because of all this financial haemorrhaging, just like the parrot in the famous Monty Python sketch, the Parrot Corporation ceased to exist, no longer living, expired, deceased, defunct, dead, an ex-parrot.

As a consequence of the aforementioned reason, I had had enough of the hi-tech electronic industry which appeared to be so transient, and ephemeral, with a *'Here today, gone tomorrow'* sort of ethos and mentality. I needed to get back into a more stable and reasonably secure well-established industry, not so evanescent and short lived as that of the kilobyte, megabyte and gigabyte world of computers and electronics which appeared to be continually in a state of flux. Innovations and changes happened so quickly in this high-speed world of electrons. In an instant, a

5

company could be the market leader, the next, on the verge of bankruptcy, having being overtaken and superseded by one of the competitors in their particular niche of the hi-tech industry.

While awaiting my turn to sign on at the Job Centre another life-changing incident transpired, sending my life spiralling off in another direction. Believe me throughout my life I had experienced a few of those incidents with a few more yet to arise in the future. This particular episode manifested itself in the form of a person named Jack Burton. From the instant of our fateful meeting, the path which my life meandered through during the next few years would ultimately take a completely different route. Cause and effect, with one event causing other events to occur later on and which, in all probability, would not have come about had I continued on the earlier, alternate life path. It has been postulated that ones passage through life is determined by ten or less major events or days in a life-time. With hindsight and upon reflection, I would not disagree with that hypothesis.

Immediately prior to encountering Jack, I had been gazing around the interior of the Job Centre, recollecting my time working in the adjacent building where the then known DHSS offices were still located and where I had once been employed, incarcerated in a small office with the attractive, intelligent and chic Myfanwy Morgan. It had been quite a few years since I last worked there during my long-haired, hippy student days in the early seventies. Those Civil Servant colleagues I once grafted alongside during those hot summer months now long since gone, either retired, deceased, promoted, changed jobs or moved on to other offices.

Jack had worked at West Mercian Oil Refineries, one of my former employers, during my time there throughout the seventies, hence the reason for us knowing each other. Ah! …West Mercian Oil, it seemed like a dream and another lifetime, a lifetime which appeared to belong to another person. As with the DHSS, it had been quite a while since I last worked there, almost ten years to be precise. *Tempus fugit,* as the saying goes.

Jack tended to be one of those very personable, garrulous individuals and whenever we bumped into each other, he invariably stopped to have a chat, wherever or whatever the situation. Being such a talkative person, he began telling me the pitiful story concerning the slow decline and downfall of West Mercian Oil Refineries and hence his reason for being at the Job Centre. He became quite loquacious, explaining in almost miniscule, pedantic detail about the refinery and the reasons for its sad demise and consequential closure.

The upshot of it was since the seventies, the whole scenario in the oil industry had changed dramatically. Oil prices nose-dived, with the recycling of industrial oils no longer proving to be the highly profitable business it had once been during the oil crisis of the mid-seventies, the decade when the price of crude oil trebled in an extremely short period of time due to the OPEC countries forming an oligopoly, or cartel using the modern day parlance. After forming the cartel, they immediately hiked the price of crude oil, holding the industrialised western world to ransom. Recycling of industrial oils had been West Mercian Oil's main business and quite lucrative when the price of crude oil remained high. Throughout the subsequent decade of the eighties, a new scenario prevailed throughout the oil industry when the price of crude oil ironically dropped due to the oil cartel falling apart, disagreeing amongst themselves as to whether they should continue with the stifling business policy of limiting the supply of crude oil and selling it at exorbitantly inflated prices. Some of the OPEC countries broke away and started selling the crude oil at lower prices as well as selling more oil to the industrialised countries by increasing their production output and hence increasing their own country's wealth. This increased world output of oil caused the price of crude oil to plummet, exacerbated by the worldwide recession taking place at the same time. The economic law of supply and demand prevailed, with the recycling or laundering of industrial oils no longer proving to be the highly attractive financial proposition it had once been in the seventies, primarily because of a glut of cheap oil now metaphorically and, almost literally, flooding the market place, causing the decline in WMO's business.

The solvent recovery side of the operation fared no better with the non-flammable, chlorinated solvents being affected by the worldwide decision to faze them out due to the adverse effects CFC's (Chloro Fluoro Carbons) appeared to be exerting upon the rapidly diminishing ozone layer. By this time, the environment and its issues began rising rapidly up the political agenda due to the increased attention given by the general population in the developed world, forcing the politicians somewhat reluctantly to act, being pushed or rather, dragged grudgingly along by vociferous public opinion, mostly environmentalists who cared about the global warming or climate change as it is referred to these days.

Due to these uncontrolled changes in the circumstances pertaining to their business and following some rather heated discussions, the decision had been taken reluctantly by the main board of Peshco, the company owning WMO, to sell off the West Mercian Oil Division to other companies.

Ultimately and unfortunately, a casualty of this financial decision turned out to be the Oil Refinery which Peshco intended to close and sell off to the highest bidder. The decision would have deeply saddened Craig Theake, the Deputy Managing Director of WMO. After all, the refinery had initially been his conception before finally emerging into the world as his new baby. Despite my unfortunate experiences in the final years with some of the latter-day managers, I felt sorry to hear about the closure of the facility where I had spent so many happy years, especially during its inception in the mid-seventies.

By now, during our rather protracted conversation, Jack informed me there could be a distinct possibility the old refinery would be taken over by a waste disposal company called Hyperwaste who intended modifying the business of the plant from oil recycling and recovery to that of a waste treatment plant, treating, or to be more precise, neutralising acids and alkalis, also chemically treating water based, soluble oils and recovering any industrial, mineral oils for burning not recycling. The plant could be deemed to be ecologically friendly, utilising waste to treat waste, alkalis to neutralise acids and also as the reagents for chemically treating the waste soluble oils.

Jack also enlightened me about Richard Cooper who had been the last Plant Manager at the refinery during its declining years. Richard had been quickly snapped up by Hyperwaste and now employed by them. The company also appeared to be on the look-out for a Site Chemist and Jack helpfully suggested I approach the Plant Manager as soon as possible, after all, as was pointed out '*nothing ventured, nothing, gained.*'

That evening I wrote a letter to the aforementioned Richard Cooper enclosing a copy of my now mushrooming CV, believing I would either hear

9

nothing more or receive yet another *Dear John* letter, so many of which I had received of late. However, within the week and much to my surprise due to the swiftness of the response, I received a reply asking me to attend an interview with Richard Cooper and Richard Mainwaring, the Regional Sales Manager.

As instructed, I attended the interview at the old refinery site, experiencing immense feelings of wistful nostalgia. It felt strange entering the old refinery where I had once worked during the seventies but which now stood eerily silent, with apparently no activity taking place within its confines. At that moment, Hyperwaste had not yet fully taken over the site and the treatment of waste materials had not yet begun in earnest.

The situation relating to my forthcoming job interview bore almost no resemblance to the circumstances of my previous interview, at that very same site, some fifteen years previous with Craig Theake. At least on this particular occasion, I could park my vehicle on solid tarmac and not in a quagmire next to a portacabin, but instead, alongside a fully completed, functioning, red brick office block. Also, in complete contrast, for this interview, the weather obligingly turned out warm, pleasant and sunny, unlike the occasion of my prior meeting, held all those aeons ago when it deemed to be misty, cold and utterly miserable.

During the intervening fifteen years since that distant interview, I had acquired a vast amount of practical experience and working knowledge concerning all sorts of hazardous waste products being used throughout industry. However, ironically enough, the only thing in common with that interview all those years ago, transpired to be the car I drove, yet another Mini, having scrapped my previous car, a Skoda

Estelle, which had mercifully expired and departed for the great scrap heap in the sky.

Fond, somewhat evocative, ghostly memories came flooding back of my time formerly spent working at the old refinery. For some inexplicably reason, almost pornographic images of Bethany, the nubile laboratory assistant, suddenly went flitting through my psyche, her enormous breasts, jutting out a fair distance from the rest of her torso, exacerbated by her tight fitting laboratory coat, giving her the appearance of a seafaring clipper in full sail. Also, not so sexually evocative memories of Anne, the other laboratory assistant, together with Dave Jarvis, Colin Hudson, Craig Theake and numerous others also went scurrying through my mind, I felt like the prodigal son returning home.

Upon surveying the old site, it became evident the storage tanks, pumps, other miscellaneous equipment and connecting pipelines appeared to be virtually the same as before, apart from a few minor additions and alterations here and there which had been made to the refinery during those intervening years.

After nervously pressing the intercom button at the doorway to the main office block, an electronically distorted voice instructed me to wait in the plush reception area. Whilst I cogitated in the waiting room, trying to relax, nervously flicking through old magazines before the forthcoming interview, another colleague from old bygone days, made a sudden and unexpected appearance.

'Hello Mucka, long time no see. How are you?'

I looked up and there stood the 5ft 10 inches, solid 16 stone frame of Jamie Soames, another one of the original process operators from the old WMO days. Jamie was yet another one of your typical, '*hail fellow, well met*,' sort of characters, very personable, bonhomie, hard to dislike and very much akin to Jack Burton. Just as one of the Process Technicians who worked for me during my time at Repeat Control Corporation, one of my former employers, referred to everyone as '*flower*,' Jamie greeted everyone with the term '*mucka*' a form of idiosyncrasy peculiar to himself. We began chatting immediately, Jamie informing me that, apart from himself, only Richard Cooper and Cedric Hughes remained at the site from the old West Mercian Oil days, the others having transferred to the main refinery in the West Midlands, found alternative jobs or, like Jack, now discovered themselves part of the growing legions of Maggie's Millions. Jamie also informed me, latterly, Cedric had been based for a few weeks in the West Midlands helping to install and commission some of the process equipment still kept by WMO and transferred to the Head Office which Peshco, hoped to keep. Although now technically working for Hyperwaste, Cedric had been allowed to work as a '*consultant*' for WMO, being paid handsomely for his work, typical Cedric ideology, anything for a few extra bob.

Jamie continued imparting more information concerning Cedric who, by this time, was well into his sixties and seemingly becoming more cantankerous and belligerent as he aged, which unfortunately sometimes appears to be a trait which accompanies the ageing process, although as far as I recalled, Cedric had always been cantankerous and aggressive, even when middle-aged. Jamie also gave me a few helpful tips for the forthcoming interview. He then shook my hand and wished me good luck before carrying on with his limited duties.

At the interview there were only three of us present - myself, Richard Cooper, the Plant Manager and Richard Mainwaring, the Area Sales Manager. The two

Richards appeared quite different physically, Richard Cooper, in his early thirties, tall, thin, lanky, dark haired and possessing a rapidly receding, hairline. I estimated him to be approximately 6 feet 5 inches tall. Later discovering he had the nickname '*Stretch,*' not because of his height, but because of some other abnormality with another more personal and intimate appendage on his anatomy, and which it seems he had once exhibited while drunk to some friends during the reception following his marriage to the gorgeous Claire, explaining, or rather slurring, to those present, all of whom exhibited more than a hint of jealousy at Richard's anatomical boon in the old wedding tackle department.

'This is what is going to do the business tonight,' he explained drunkenly, with more than a hint of personal pride at the unique, enhanced size of his genitalia.

Later, I discovered Richard Cooper's mother Pat, turned out to be the very same Pat working on the switchboard at Birchwater, during my altercation with Dean Crabbe.

Conversely and the complete antithesis, the other Richard, also in his early thirties resembled Billy Bunter, the old television and comic character, that is to say short and dumpy, sporting a huge mop of dark brown hair, peering at me through huge, brown rimmed spectacles. The two Richards were in fact the long and the short of it.

From the outset, I had the distinct feeling, the interview went very well, appearing to impress both interviewers with my knowledge of oil water separation, the cracking of soluble oils, enhanced by my working knowledge of chemical analytical techniques using Gas Chromatography, Atomic Absorption, Infra-red Spectra photometry, titration procedures knowledge of different chemicals such as cyanide, chromic acid, a plethora of solvents, all my chemical experience and knowledge coming to the fore, which would be invaluable when working in the hazardous waste industry. They also appeared interested in my practical Chemical Engineering knowledge concerning pumps, filtration systems, particularly filter presses, settlement equipment, storage tanks, pipe installations and a whole range of other process engineering related topics, knowledge mainly acquired during my time with Repeat Controls Corporation. After they had asked me some technical questions, I asked them mine, the obligatory subjects, mostly concerned with pay, hours, holidays, pensions etc.

Finally, the interview came to an end, with Richard Mainwaring enquiring if I had anything pressing that day and if possible, would I wait in the reception area for a short time. Informing them I had nothing planned for the remainder of the day and able to remain on the site as long as they wished, I returned to the reception area and waited as instructed.

Within twenty minutes they both came out, offering me the position then and there, enquiring if I could commence work the following week. I accepted their offer, despite the relatively low remuneration on offer. As referred to earlier, this job would eventually propel me down an entirely new route in life, very different to the Hi-tech world. Little did I realize at the time what a journey it would eventually turn out to be! Yes, this plant definitely seemed to be lucky for me, working there on two separate occasions for two different companies.

The following Monday I began working for my new employer at the old familiar site. The initial weeks primarily spent setting up the laboratory, installing the sophisticated analytical equipment, putting them into position and connecting the narrow copper pipelines for the gases required to operate the equipment. Richard Mainwaring had ordered the new analytical equipment and my main objective involved setting the new laboratory up as quickly as possible. Small quantities of soluble and dirty mineral oils began arriving in tankers for treatment. I worked closely with Jamie in determining the optimum treatment for cracking the soluble oils using ferric chloride, calcium chloride, alkali, and polyelectrolyte. Standard chemicals used for the 'cracking' of stable oil emulsions. After I had calculated the full scale amount of chemicals required, Jamie then added them to the soluble oils in the treatment tank.

During those initial weeks, the curmudgeonly Cedric Hughes eventually made his re-appearance on the site. It surprised me how the years had indeed made him even more belligerent than previous. He had been bad enough in the old days with WMO, but had now transformed into a real Victor Meldrew but even more so contemptuous and opinionated, with extremely bigoted, xenophobic, objectionable attitudes towards almost anything, Blacks, Jews, Arabs, Irish, Scots, English, Americans, French, Gays, the whole spectrum. You name it, he had something derogatory to say about the subject being discussed and which he put forward in a dogmatic, unyielding attitude, continually using Anglo-Saxon expletives repetitively in every sentence, being a person of somewhat limited vocabulary.

An obvious antagonism and antipathy existed between Jamie and Cedric, with both vying for the attention, approbation and patronage of Richard Cooper. Unsurprisingly really, for Cedric appeared to be in competition with the whole world.

Notwithstanding Cedric, I enjoyed those early days at Hyperwaste returning to the old memorable site, recalling the fond memories of days gone by. My early weeks throughout July and August of 1989, mostly spent setting up the laboratory, installing the state of the art, brand new chemical analytical equipment which Richard Mainwaring had already purchased.

The days tended to be totally laid back and easy going, interrupted occasionally with the arrival of the sporadic tanker loads of waste oils arriving on site.

Once the laboratory equipment had been finally installed, the rest of the time I spent analysing waste materials which the sales representatives continually brought in. Periodically, the company Sales Representatives from other Hyperwaste depots appeared on site and put samples of all sorts of disgusting materials on my desk and then brusquely remark.

'Can you tell me what it is and what it contains?'

I had a terrible job explaining to them I did not have a full forensic laboratory set up with the capability of analysing for every material known to man on the planet, but very limited capabilities in the types of analysis I could perform with the analytical equipment available. However, after discussing the client and the industry they tended to be involved with, I always tried to give them some idea of what I believed the materials contained for them to arrange the appropriate legal disposal site. If they were oils, then we allowed them to be disposed of on the site.

I was thoroughly enjoying myself, but should have known it was too good to last, as unknown to me, ominous, dark clouds of impending upheaval, instability and turmoil loomed large on the horizon.

CHAPTER 2

*W*est Mercian Oil had previously operated the old site as a recycling plant mainly for mineral oils and non-flammable, chlorinated solvents. The treatment and disposal of water-based, synthetic oils, which the company also carried out, manifested itself as a side-line, an additional service for the regular, high-volume, high paying customers. An agreement between WMO and the local Waste Disposal Authority, at the behest of the latter's paymasters, that is to say, the local Council, allowed this additional treatment process without the requirement of a waste disposal licence, mainly because of the overall nature and predominant business operation being carried out on the site. As far as the Council was concerned, WMO was not treating but recycling and returning the oils and solvents to the customers, basically a laundry service for these materials. Besides they wanted to encourage the company to situate their refinery in the area and not put too many legal obstacles in their way. Hence WMO did not require a waste treatment licence for the site. This gentleman's agreement deferring the need of a Waste Licence for the refinery regarding this additional operation for the treatment and disposal of soluble, synthetic oils would have disastrous ramifications when it came to Hyperwaste's investment plans, now some years down the line.

The new company, fully intended using the site as a waste treatment plant, primarily for the treatment of soluble oils, also taking in waste acids and alkalis, which would then be used neutralise each other. In reality, proving to be an excellent ecological proposition, utilising waste in order to neutralise waste. No laundering and recycling of oils would take place. Any mineral oils received on the premises would then be re-sold as cheap fuel oil to feed the huge industrial boilers dispersed throughout the United Kingdom.

There was, however, one major obstacle to this intended business venture. Plans had been approved to locate a prominent Garden Festival exhibition in the area. The layout for the site indicated this prestigious horticultural event would eventually completely surround and envelope the existing treatment plant. It was not going to be very good advertising or PR for the organises of the Garden Festival to have a hazardous waste treatment plant slap bang in the middle of their prestigious, highly publicised European tourism project, intended to last well over twelve months. Because of its very nature, the waste treatment operation would invariably necessitate 20 tonne tankers trundling right through the festival site to reach the gates of the treatment facility, and those vehicles would be fully loaded with, oil, acid or caustic soda. However, the main over-riding, covert factor and unpublished objections against Hyperwaste using the plant as a waste treatment facility came from some of the local Councillors, with a few of them later hoping to cash in on future plans for a proposed housing development, which would invariably follow the closure of the exhibition. Ultimately, the previously highly polluted land could later be developed upon after the area had been completely chemically decontaminated with money so generously provided by the EU in preparation for the esteemed exhibition. A few unscrupulous champagne-socialist Councillors fully intended lining their greasy palms with filthy lucre as huge British pound signs appeared before their covetous eyes at the thought of the new housing

18

development and getting into bed with some high-flying property developers. The unprincipled, amoral, greedy councillors saw an opportunity of harnessing the antagonism of the local community, by stimulating protests and generating a vast amount of hostile media attention against the proposed waste treatment plant and ultimately eliminating the problem of a treatment plant still being there in the middle a new planned housing development a few years ahead.

Battle lines had now been drawn, with all combatants firmly entrenched. Hyperwaste verses the local community, supported by the local council and the Welsh Development Agency. A reverse scenario from the days when West Mercian Oil established their refinery on the derelict site, being actively pursued, wooed, cajoled and encouraged by previous Councillors in establishing their refinery on heavily contaminated land which nobody wanted anything to do with at that time. Now circumstances had altered dramatically with the distinct possibility of huge amounts of money to be made in the future.

Unfortunately, not for the first time during my career time-line, I discovered myself unintentionally caught in the middle of a political conflagration between local residents, the local Council and a large company. The Waste Disposal Authority at the time reported directly to the Council and unfortunately their paymasters. A few years later, this situation altered when the disposal of waste came under the national Environment Agency, but at that time in the late eighties and beginning of the nineties, the local Waste Disposal Authority controlled all matters relating to hazardous waste within the region however, as mentioned, not completely autonomous but subject to the whims, peccadilloes and instructions, of the Councillors.

In September 1989, the local Council, instructed the Waste Disposal Authority to refuse permission for the company to accept any more waste. Almost immediately the litigious battle commenced in earnest, much to the glee and profuse rubbing of hands on the part of solicitors, barristers and anyone concerned with the legal establishment, whichever side of the fence they transpired to be placed, with both legal teams standing to gain substantially from the forthcoming high profile and ultimately long drawn out legal encounter.

Paradoxically, for the time being, my job was relatively secure. Hyperwaste had to prove they had competent, technical people on site so kept all of us employed during the legally imposed embargo and closure. Although not allowed to take in waste or even process or treat the waste we had stored on the site, I still had a multitude of other tasks to perform, such as getting analytical procedures set in place and all the systems for paperwork etc., also analysing wastes for the representatives as Hyperwaste was a rapidly expanding company with depots all over the country, becoming a sort of '*technical chemical guru*' for the UK, receiving phone calls from people throughout the country concerning all sorts of chemicals and chemical cleaning operations, asking my advice on how to dispose of various materials and the best disposal sites to use for the plethora of chemical wastes and the possible reactions between the different types of materials. If I did not know the answer, I made further enquiries to determine the answer or remedy and report back. I acquired a tremendous amount of knowledge about disposal of waste, the best and cheapest disposal sites to use which proliferated the country, gaining extensive knowledge as to the types of wastes each disposal site was permitted to handle, together with carriage and transportation of the chemical wastes and the new legal requirements which had to be adhered to. Also the proper waste identification on tankers and the optimum type of tanker required for the shipment of a particular hazardous material. I also advised on the installation of the new process equipment and having a wonderful time, enjoying every minute, shame about the low salary on offer though.

Meanwhile, the unrequited, unwanted media attention began increasing together with the frequency of demonstrations. One morning, after leaving the site for a couple of hours, upon returning discovered the gates of the plant blocked by a mob of angry, fist-waving, banner-wielding demonstrators. Amongst the throng some of the prominent, unscrupulous Councillors, previously alluded to, trying to remain inconspicuous. With my entrance inhibited by the throng, whilst driving slowly past the angry, confrontational, belligerent horde, the wheels of my small Mini car almost went over the rather large, protruding feet of the local MP, who had succeeded Michael Foot as the representative for local constituency in the House of Commons.

From personal experience, I considered those to be fun, exciting days, as one never knew what was going to happen from one day to the next, while in work or, for that matter, before going into work. Such as the one particular occasion, before commencing my working day, upon arriving at the site discovering the gates had been chained and padlocked, both the padlock and chain being quite substantial in size and extremely difficult to remove. All the other personnel working on site had abandoned their vehicles outside the main gates. Looking out from my car towards the portacabin which doubled as the canteen and mess room, I observed my work colleagues gesticulating from the comfort and warmth of their safe-haven for me to clamber over the immense gates. Meanwhile two men from the local newspaper stood outside the gates of the plant, a cub reporter and photographer. From the outset, the local rag, had sided with the demonstrators, becoming strongly anti-Hyperwaste and whole-heartedly throwing their weight behind the local action committee. It being November, the weather was, as usual, inclement, extremely cold, wet and absolutely miserable.

The previous evening, the Editor of the newspaper had received an anonymous telephone call. During the subsequent conversation the caller suggested it would be a prudent action on the Editor's part to send one of his reporters and a photographer to the plant gates for 6:00 in the morning and acquire a journalistic scoop. However, the editor had no knowledge of the fact, but we did not actually commence work until 08:00. Hence, the two unfortunate journalists turned up at the gates at 5:30 as instructed by their boss, in the hope of obtaining a newspaper revelation which could possibly propel them and the paper into the big time. Because of the cold weather, the poor journalists were absolutely frozen. As directed by my colleagues, in the portacabin, I clambered over the substantially padlocked gates, the reporter, note book poised in hand, began, firing questions at me, desperately attempting to take notes with the biro just about held in his white, frozen fingers of his right hand. Although by this time he probably thought his fingers actually belonged to someone else, having no feeling in them whatsoever.

'What is your job on site?' he asked in his best investigative journalistic style, through chattering teeth.

'My official job title is "Plant Chemist,"' I replied breathlessly, while at the same time desperately struggling to pull my right leg over the top of the huge gates.

'And what does that actually entail?' the cub reporter persisted, trying to emulate Jeremy Paxman in an aggressive style of interrogation.

'Well.....' I replied, carefully formulating my response so as not to land myself or the company well and truly in it, while at the same time gasping for air through my rapidly overworked lungs. By this time, I precariously straddled the top of the tall gates, with my legs on either side of the metal barrier. I then continued with my answers to this impromptu and unwanted interview.

'During the break periods, I go around the site with a small trolley selling condoms, aspirins, shampoo and toothpaste.'

The reporter, assiduously, with an almost religious fervour began writing all my comments down, verbatim. Suddenly he stopped, thought a second, before realizing he had been well and truly wound up. As he glared up at me, I looked back down at him, exhibiting an almost cherubic smile before slowly sliding down the other side of the gate safely ensconced within the confines of the treatment plant.

'Any chance of a coffee, we've been here since six and we're both frozen?' enquired the photographer, who, seconds earlier, had been frantically clicking away with his expensive camera, taking numerous photos of me in all sorts of undignified positions, while I had desperately clambered over what, at the time, seemed like the north face of the Eiger.

'I'll see what I can do,' I replied, taking pity on them both. After all, they were only doing their jobs.

Upon entering the portacabin containing the mess room, I discovered Richard Cooper, Jamie and Cedric together with the guys from the garage and the fabricating contractor working on site. All had miscellaneous, steaming, hot beverages comprising of coffee, tea or soup, contained in huge mugs clutched in their hands.

'Struggled a bit getting over the gates there didn't you, Mucka? You could do with losing a few pounds,' remarked Jamie sarcastically.

'Pot, kettle, black, springs to mind,' I replied, before finally reluctantly agreeing with him.

'Yeah I did a bit. It didn't help with those bastards asking me questions and taking photos at the same time.'

'They did it to us all,' added Cedric in his usual morose, stroppy manner.

'They asked if there was any chance we would give them a cup of coffee,' I mentioned hesitantly.

'Well they can piss off!' chirped in Richard Cooper who had been sitting quietly in the corner of the mess cabin perusing over some paperwork.

Despite all of his bravado and portrayed animosity, Richard went out later that morning with two, hot, steaming mugs of coffee for the two journalists, his philosophy being '*Well there is no point in trying to antagonize the press it may work against you.*' Besides, it was against his nature to be nasty or vindictive.

The padlock and chains on the gate being huge, it took the contractors some considerable period of time to cut one of the links with their oxy–acetylene equipment in order to open the gates, enabling access to the site.

Yes, those were certainly fun days with the demonstrators suddenly appearing in front of the gates at the drop of a hat, their banners and placards lofted high in the air with the local TV cameras and newspaper reporters in tow, the whole media circus, an almost obligatory part of such controversial projects.

I recall one particular day friendly waving back at the demonstrators, only to have a Harvey Smith two fingers riposte in reply. The cameras zoomed onto my face which appeared that evening on the local television news of both ITV and BBC. There I was, quite happily waving to a Harvey Smith, two-finger salute, like 'the village idiot' which is how Ioan Davies, one of the local depot Managers, described me. I looked like a pillock waving friendly and smiling at an obviously belligerent and angry person. Although heaven help me had I given a two-finger salute back.

Despite all the prohibitions put on the treatment of waste at the former refinery, Hyperwaste continued with their expansion plans, having new process equipment and buildings installed which they were legally entitled to do, having previously and erroneously been given planning permission by the planning department of the local council, someone in that office had dropped a bollock by giving permission.

Because of the political situation, my duties became amended. It was decided I would be better utilized actually sorting out waste materials for packaging, identification and shipment at customer premises. For a couple of weeks I received instructions and coaching from Malcolm Roundtree, one of the technical representatives, on how to correctly package the chemicals and label the containers for shipment. Malcolm intended leaving the company for loftier things and there was a large contract up in Carlisle with the MOD, which I had been instructed to supervise, so I needed an instructional crash course on the modified proper packaging procedure and labelling, ensuring conformity to the new regulations for the transportation and shipment of small amounts of hazardous waste and ultimate disposal ensuring conformity to the specific disposal site's stipulated requirements.

Malcolm departed from Hyperwaste at the end of December 1989. Then in January 1990, the company despatched me to the MOD establishment in Carlisle as his replacement. The site was a maintenance depot for the MOD and materials had been shipped back from all over the world such as paints solvents acids alkalis. My task mainly consisted of sorting it all out for shipment to Shanks at Stewartby located near Bedford. I spent about two weeks up at the facility working with Daniel Chivers, one of the managers from a local haulage company with whom Hyperwaste had jointly set up the contract. During the project, it became evident the MOD was a law unto itself. Daniel and I wished to consult with the local Waste Disposal Authority concerning some technical aspects of the project. The camp commander told us in no uncertain terms, he had no wish for any regulatory bodies to set foot in the camp, hinting the site had some depleted uranium stored on the site which he no wish to make public. He therefore prohibited the WDA visiting the site in case they accidentally discovered the illegal material on site, also pointing out he had the authority to do so.

I recollect at the time, the UK was being ravaged by gales and floods. I was up north during the week when the weather tended to be quite mild and pleasant. However, the weather in Wales was horrendous. Upon returning to South Wales for the weekend, the exact opposite occurred, gales occurring up north whilst Wales experienced the milder weather. I went back up north and once again the opposite. I was forever missing the horrendous conditions, probably my reward for leading a clean and pure life. I did enjoy travelling up and being left on my own, driving for hours in my own company. Stella did not seem to mind my absences too much with me travelling around the country. We had been living together for almost two years by now so it was not as if we were newlyweds. I was getting to be an expert in waste disposal techniques thanks to Hyperwaste. It was a case of sink or swim.

Finally, the project reached completion and went very well. Everyone involved seemed pleased with the outcome.

I enjoyed those times with Hyperwaste. Being away interspersed with time spent at the treatment plant performing routine chemical analysis or on the phone answering technical, chemical questions from the transport managers and chemical cleaning operations based in throughout the UK. Any periods of boredom at the plant tended to be interspersed and alleviated by the previously mentioned angry placard waving demonstrators, all extremely exciting and thoroughly enjoyable.

Apart from the quarrelsome Cedric, everyone worked well together. There is no denying it, he did have one hell of an attitude problem.

The refinery ended up being situated at the top corner of the now rapidly proliferating Festival site and positioned in a cul-de-sac. Large, articulated vehicles came to the top end, emptying their loads for the exhibition. With the approach road being so narrow, many drivers used the refinery as a sort of turning circle. Most of us had no problem with this. After all it was not an easy job driving a 40 feet articulated vehicle and we understood the drivers' attempt at making their job as easy as possible. Cedric, however, took a different viewpoint, considered it his duty to put a stop to what he considered uncouth and completely yobbish drivers, using the beckoning vastness of the refinery in which to turn their immense vehicles.

One driver had just off-loaded a load of straw and availed himself of the welcoming, expanse of the refinery in which to turn his huge articulated vehicle.

27

Cedric, upon observing the driver making, what he considered unauthorised use of the Refinery facilities, ran out to stop him, dashing out in front of the vehicle, his action verging on being almost suicidal. As he jumped in front the articulated vehicle, the driver braked sharply to prevent his vehicle running over the maniacal Engineer, almost propelling him through the windscreen of the cab. Now there are ways of instructing people and informing them politely what they should or should not do, it is known as *tact*. However, the word '*tact*' appeared to be a word completely alien to Cedric and not part of his somewhat limited, Anglo-Saxon vocabulary. He immediately began hurling a torrent of abuse and profanity at the rather bemused lorry driver. 'I'm fed up of telling you fucking lorry drivers. You are not allowed to turn your vehicles in this refinery. This is private property, you arsehole!'

The driver's perplexed appearance quickly transformed into anger and loathing for this little Hitler now standing in front of his beloved vehicle and who incessantly ranted and raved at him.

Slowly and purposely the driver emerged from the confines of his warm cab and descended the metal steps. Cedric gulped heavily as this giant of a man now towered above his somewhat diminutive 5 ft. 5 inch frame becoming transfixed and mesmerised like a rabbit caught in the beam of car headlights as this leviathan approached. An obvious mixture of anger, contempt and intense loathing now exuded from the driver's narrowing eyes. He was a huge man, well over 6ft 5 inches and almost 20 stone, your typical, hairy-arsed, corpulent lorry driver, wearing torn jeans, which appeared to be barely supported by his huge waist which hung over his belt, the latter being completely enveloped and hidden by a mass of flesh. He also sported a heavily, somewhat fetching, grubby and tea-stained vest displaying a large amount of tattoos over most visible parts of his sweaty, hairy body and looked as if he had not shaved for a few days. His face exuded complete menace and malevolence. It became evident almost immediately, to everyone in the vicinity this was most definitely not a man to be messed with. It also dawned upon Cedric that he had unquestionably picked upon the wrong driver to berate in such an aggressive manner.

The driver slowly and deliberately walked right up to the, now, utterly terrified Cedric and when in close proximity immediately began prodding the diminutive engineer quite forcefully in the chest, using the rather large index finger of his right hand as the implement of torture. The driver prodded Cedric as he spoke, with each prod the engineer recoiled backwards.

'If I want to turn my fucking,' *prod*, 'vehicle,' *prod*' I'll turn my fucking' *prod* 'vehicle'

'I don't,' *prod* 'care who the hell,' *prod* 'you' *prod* 'are.' *prod*

Cedric's pallor and demeanour now changed rapidly.

'Just informing you that's all mate,' he squeaked back in reply, his voice now raising an octave or two higher. No expletives from Cedric this time, his tone becoming distinctly more conciliatory and rather subservient in nature. The driver grunted a form of acknowledgement to Cedric's high pitched answer, giving an extremely good impression of a Neanderthal man. After grunting his response, the driver slowly returned to his cab and completed the turning exercise of his articulated vehicle, this time, without any further hindrance from the traumatised Maintenance Engineer.

Jamie could not resist having a word with Cedric after the vehicle vacated the plant gates at speed, closely followed by an attendant cloud of dust.

'I hope you told him off Cedric?' he enquired with more than a hint of his usual sarcasm, while at the same time desperately trying to stifle a snigger.

Cedric not realizing the incident had been observed quite so closely, replied.

'Yeah I gave him a right ear bashing. I told the bastard!' he lied, unashamedly.

Jamie exhibiting a broad smile, replied,

'Yeah I heard you. You certainly told him alright.'

Cedric was obviously shaken and embarrassed by the whole episode returning quickly to the anodyne sanctuary of his office. Everyone, including myself, had a snigger at Cedric's obvious unease with the whole experience.

Towards the end of 1989, about the same time the Berlin wall was being dismantled with unabashed enthusiasm, other metaphorical walls were being erected with as much zeal, with Hyperwaste becoming even more heavily embroiled in its own battle against the Council and the local action committee led by a certain harridan and battle-axe named Amelia Thomas. Amelia and her servile husband lived in a small village in the vicinity of the site. However, despite being the nearest village to the plant, it tended to be still quite a distance away from the source of their animosity. Mrs Thomas had stirred up and manipulated the local residents, forming an action committee, egged on, as previously mentioned, by some rather dubious Councillors, who allegedly were heavily involved with some local builders and construction companies. They gave Mrs. Thomas the bullets, but stayed in the background not wishing to look as if they were actively involved, only wanting the land around the Hyperwaste site for the future housing development. A waste treatment plant in the middle of their proposed new housing development would be do nothing to help their plans in selling the new yuppie houses to prospective buyers, and they wanted nothing to hinder their intentions of making large amounts of money. The literature distributed by the action committee, tended to be, to say the least, totally misleading and completely inaccurate. All the plant intended to treat was oil, interceptor waters, acids, and waste alkalis mainly from steelworks and electroplating plants disposing of the untreated waste in the proper authorised manner.

According to the highly flawed, misleading literature and leaflets being distributed by the action committee, Hyperwaste fully intended using the site for treating radioactive materials which Sellafield could not deal with, pesticides and polychlorinated biphenyls (PCB) which the, two state of the art, high temperature incineration facilities based at Pontypool and Ellesmere Port allegedly could not handle, together with all sorts of miscellaneous toxic materials such as arsenic, asbestos, cadmium, mercury and cyanide which landfill sites could not take throughout the UK. In short the plant would take in all sorts of unwanted, waste chemicals not capable of being treated or disposed of elsewhere in the UK or even the world, for that matter, which was far removed from the truth. The site was for oil, water, acid, alkali treatment, nothing more, nothing less.

Unfortunately to exacerbate the situation, bad press was also being heaped on the Hyperwaste's Chairman, Samuel Abbott, to such an extent he became the main topic of a *This Week Special* on ITV which did nothing to help the company, the programme bestowing him with the title of, '*The Toxic Playboy,*' accusing him of previously being involved with 'fly tipping' after becoming Managing Director of another waste company, following his marriage to the owner's daughter, courting her while working for the company as a driver. The inference being the marriage only came about because of his wife's wealth and a desire on his part to obtain a seat on the board of directors, basically, accusing him of being your bog standard 'gold-digger.' The TV programme deliberately showed his huge mansion in the outback and wilds of Surrey transmitting the programme throughout the UK. At one point, the programme showed Samuel Abbott risibly desperately trying to evade questioning by the tenacious reporter and filming by the cameraman whilst out on his early morning jog. He appeared ridiculous as he refused to answer questions, desperately attempted to evade the unrelenting pursuing reporter like a chicken attempting to escape a pursuing, hungry fox. Following the media fiasco with Samuel Abbott, the French Multinational decided to make the position of Chairman redundant, firing both Samuel Abbott and Dave Parry the original MD. Once they had been removed from the company, Hyperwaste came under the complete leadership of Tom Driscoll.

Up until this time the company had remained fairly quiet when it came to talking to the press and holding dialogue with the demonstrators. This policy changed dramatically when Tom Driscoll became MD. He decided upon a new, contrasting strategy to his predecessors, inviting the local action committee to the site and showing them around, together with members of the council and the local WDA, who were well-acquainted with the site in their official capacity. Hyperwaste also invited Jane O'Brien the local Chief Reporter from the regional newspaper, a rather attractive, petite thirty year old brunette, who had been writing unflattering articles about the site and the company.

We all sat around the table like two belligerent warring tribes, while Helen, Richard's secretary, efficiently and unobtrusively dished out the sandwiches. Dave Moreland, the Regional Area Sales Director, began flirting outrageously with Jane. From the outset, it became evident his charms had been completely wasted on the hard, po-faced, ice-cold and probably frigid Amelia Thomas, the action committee chairperson. Amelia had one objective and one objective only, the complete closure of the site. No amount of compliments and '*soft soaping*' from an ageing Lothario were going to detract her from the main objective. So after a rebuff from Amelia, Dave Moreland aimed his charms at Jane, who was younger and far more attractive than the prematurely ageing committee chairperson. Dave adopted the premise get the press on your side. Jane reciprocated wholeheartedly with the flirting as there obviously appeared to be a chemistry and mutual attraction between the two of them.

After the bun fight, we all went for a walk around the site as Dave explained to the committee and the councillors, how Hyperwaste intended to develop the site and treat the wastes in the proper manner adhering to all legislative requirements, then asking myself or Richard Cooper for any technical details he found himself unable to answer.

Where Dave Moreland had failed to charm the aloof, impenetrable Amelia Thomas, Richard Cooper thought he would have a crack, only to be met with the same stony-faced response from the inscrutable committee Chairperson.

I later discovered Amelia Thomas worked in a factory which used a large amount of hazardous,

33

chemicals, including flammable and toxic solvents, some far more lethal, toxic and dangerous than the chemicals we intended to treat. I thought hypocritical in the circumstances considering the chemicals we intended to treat were waste oils and low concentration spent acids and spent alkalis.

During the walkabout, both Dave and Richard Cooper became so involved talking with their numerous guests, they failed to notice Cedric trying his ancient charms on the voluptuous Jane

O'Brien. Despite being in his sixties, Cedric was still a lecherous old git, continually trying it on with younger women despite the fact they were out of his league in culture, sophistication and more importantly, age.

Dave enquired in passing where Cedric had disappeared to. We looked back only to observe the Maintenance Engineer in the distance chatting to Jane and within quite close proximity to the female journalist, appearing to be worryingly attempting to manoeuvre his right arm around her slim, lithe waist and obviously desperately inflicting his limited charms on the young reporter. Dave looked at me and I detected more than a slight hint of panic and horror in his face. Whispering so as not to be overheard, he spoke to me. 'What is he saying to her? Vinson, go and separate them both before he says something which will land us all in the shit and before we have an attempted rape charge on our hands!'

I could not help smiling to myself, for I knew Cedric of old, during his time with West Mercian Oil and how he often lusted after both Beth and Anne, the two, nubile laboratory assistants, resembling Cosmo Smallpiece, the Les Dawson character. The last thing Hyperwaste needed was to be at the centre of an attempted rape charge by their Maintenance Engineer after he had pounced on the Chief Reporter of the local newspaper.

I believe Dave had visions of the headlines blazoned on the front page with the obligatory newspaper pun, composed by Jane herself.

'HOW I WAS SCREWED BY HYPERWASTE'S MAINTENANCE ENGINEER'

Or perhaps:

'MY SHOCKING ORDEAL AT THE HANDS OF HYPERWASTE'S ELECTRICAL

ENGINEER'

Dave fully realised the power of the press and how the pen is indeed mightier than the sword.

I quickly ran to separate Cedric from the female reporter. Cedric could not understand why I wanted to extricate him from the attractive reporter. I lied brazenly, informing him Dave Moreland wanted to talk to Jane about the operation of the plant, which seemed to placate him somewhat. After that incident, both Dave Moreland and Richard Cooper made certain Cedric remained well away from the local newspaper's Chief Reporter.

The meeting ended with the Waste Disposal Authority being fairly conciliatory, however, before she left, Amelia Thomas made it abundantly clear she would only be satisfied when the plant was completely shut down. Meanwhile her husband and the rest of the committee hardly said a word. The few Councillors present hardly spoke, but we all knew, they wanted the plant, if possible completely eviscerated mostly for their own grasping, greedy desires.

There is a post script to these events. During the new millennium, I decided one day to tune into the BBC News 24 Channel, only to hear the anchorman say 'And now we go to our Washington Correspondent, Jane O' Brien.'

Evidently, the whole Hyperwaste experience obviously did the female reporter no harm whatsoever in her ambition to advance her journalistic career.

CHAPTER 3

*T*he facility at the treatment plant had plenty of vacant space available, both outside and inside. In the very early days, only Richard Cooper, Helen Jones, Richard's new secretary and I tended to be ensconced in the main office block with plenty of space in which to rattle around. During the earlier heydays of West Mercian Oil Refineries, all of the eight offices had been fully utilised with lots of people coming and going throughout the building during the day, the building a bustling hive of activity. Now the offices tended to be quite empty and ghostly silent, except when the occasional visitor came to the site.

I had only been working at the facility for a couple of months when a new face appeared on the scene, in the rather large, imposing figure of Fred Germaine who could only be described as your typical genial, worldly-wise Londoner, with the south east London semi-cockney accent, much like Jamie Soames, hail fellow well met with a *bonhomie* attitude and could certainly *not* be describe as reserved or quiet. He had lived in South Wales for a number of years, in a very select and posh area of a South Wales holiday resort, Porthcawl, better known as '*hi butty bay.*' It became a place popular with people from the South Wales valleys and where they gravitated towards, particularly during the bank holidays, annual vacation and weekends heading specifically towards the amusement park and the caravan park at Trecco Bay. The holidaymakers frequently bumped into their friends or neighbours, hence the name 'Hi Butty Bay' developed.

Fred had been in the Merchant Navy for a number of years, having worked his way up through the ranks, rising to the responsible position of Ship's Captain, navigating large tankers for BP around the seven seas. His attractive wife hailed from South Wales hence the reason why they both now resided in that well-known seaside resort. I must admit to enjoying Fred's sense of humour, he always had a smile and a joke or humorous quip to impart, which helped the long days pass that much quicker. We all liked Fred who being in his 50's was another person possessing a degree from the *University of Life and Existentialism*, frequently imparting an anecdote or two about his time spent sailing the oceans. He had a very thorough knowledge about chemicals and their hazardous properties, particularly when it came to highly inflammable solvents such as methanol and ethanol.

After joining the local golf club near to his home in Porthcawl, Fred became friendly with Dave Parry, the then Managing Director of Hyperwaste. Following a few conversations with Dave, Fred made it abundantly clear he was seeking employment. Dave offered him a position within the company, with the dual role of Safety Officer/Quality Manager helping implement safe working procedures and also set up the new ISO 5740 Quality standard for documentation systems which the company wanted to be able to print on the headed note paper as a status symbol. At that time, not many companies possessed the much sought after prestigious certificate and accompanying logo.

The journey from Porthcawl to the treatment plant of approximately 50 miles added to Fred's working day by at least 2 hours, but Fred was happy enough to accept the post, as the job came with a company car, a white Diesel Peugeot 405 and all fuel paid for by his employer.

We often listened, totally enthralled and captivated by Fred's tales of his time spent in the merchant navy working for BP and his voyages around the world travelling to glamorous, exotic locations, particularly the Middle and Far East, with stories of being invited aboard luxurious yachts belonging to rich Sheiks in the Gulf, where he consumed fascinating, strange, colourful meals and partake in other diversions. Also about the inherent dangers present when shipping vast amounts of highly flammable and dangerous liquids around the globe.

As the days turned into months, Fred began spending more and more time away from the plant, visiting other Hyperwaste depots scattered throughout the UK, helping to set up safety procedures and also implementing the new Quality systems. He also had to attend various courses, despite his vast knowledge and experience, Fred had no formal qualifications in the two responsible jobs he had taken on. So the company considered it prudent to put him onto some relevant courses and pretty damn quickly at that.

It soon became evident Fred possessed the tendency of always being late attending meetings and not being places he should be at any particular time. Not a good example for an ex-ship's Captain and Quality Manager. If he looked likely of being excessively late or in a hurry when driving on the motorway and the traffic appeared to be moving far too slowly in the fast lane for his liking. Fred would deliberately pull over at the most convenient exit, don his hi-visibility, yellow coat, get back into his car and return to the highway. He then intentionally drove down the fast lane, any car he found barring his way, he would rapidly flash his car headlights at. The impeding driver in front of him, upon looking in his rear view mirror, and observing a brand new white Peugeot, with flashing headlights, its occupant wearing a yellow hi-visibility jacket, would immediately come to the erroneous conclusion he had a police car on his tail. The car, which inevitably tended to be exceeding the legal limit, would immediately go into the middle lane and reduce his speed. Other cars would automatically do the same thing. Suddenly there, ahead of him, Fred had the desired spectacle of an unrestricted fast lane of the motorway. Although he did not actually impersonate a police officer, he came pretty damn close to it. But he never once got stopped by a legitimate police car. This little subterfuge of Fred's usually speeded up his journey quite considerably, making up for any lost time.

Whenever Fred made his, by now, infrequent visits to the site, he always had some adventure or mishap to relate to us all, which made his visits to the plant all the more enjoyable and memorable. I recall the day he came in uttering oaths and expletives concerning the driving ability and behaviour of BMW Drivers and one BMW driver in particular. Fred had been travelling on the motorway making his way from Porthcawl to the treatment plant. During the journey he had been cut up quite violently and sharply by a BMW. I do not know the model as Fred was not forthcoming on that information.

The action of the driver had infuriated Fred. In return, he speeded up and did exactly the same to the other driver that is to say, cutting up the BMW in much the same aggressive manner.

This was road rage, and in the early nineties, a fairly new phenomenon. Fred went on to explain how both drivers persisted with this rather childish behaviour for some time as he and his new found adversary kept cutting each other up a considerable number of miles along the motorway.

Finally Fred, who I must admit to personally, finding generally an easy going sort of person, lost his temper. He began gesticulating to the driver of the BMW for them both to pull over onto the hard shoulder of the motorway where they could sort out their differences *mano et mano.*

The driver of the BMW acquiesced to Fred's demands, pulling over onto the hard shoulder, of the motorway as agreed. The reader may correct me if I am mistaken but I don't think that is written anywhere in the highway code that drivers may pull over onto the hard shoulder of a bustling motorway in order to knock six bells out of each other. I believe it may even be considered illegal. Notwithstanding this minor point of law, Fred pulled his Peugeot in front of the gleaming, almost brand new feat of German engineering.

I should perhaps describe Fred who presented quite an imposing figure measuring in at about 6 feet 5 inches tall, 18 stone and built like a Russian T34 tank, quite muscular, possessing not an ounce of flab. As Fred related his story, I imagined the look of horror on the face of that BMW driver as he observed the spectacle of this enormous man slowly and deliberately emerging from his Peugeot 405. At the end of his monologue, he asked me rhetorically,

'You'll never guess what the bastard did when I started walking towards his car?'

'Let me Guess!' I replied, even though I knew Fred was not expecting an answer to his question.

'Did he drive off at high speed by any chance?' I enquired nonchalantly.

Fred looked at me quizzically, not realising how his immense frame appeared to other people, particularly when he exhibited a scowl or angry demeanour, and how terrifying he could look at times.

'Yeah, how did you know?'

'Just a lucky guess,' I replied with a huge smile on my face adding the statement,

'You just can't trust BMW Drivers, arrogant bastards!'

With that final assertion, I walked off, still smiling to myself.

Fred, despite being the safety officer had at least three car crashes that I am aware of during his time with Hyperwaste. Not a good record for someone who is supposed to be in charge of safety for the company. In his defence however, I must say that in all three accidents, it was the other driver who was at fault.

He had to set the quality system up at the Treatment plant, to his credit, became wholeheartedly committed to setting up the paperwork system. The only problem being, he had to discuss the ISO Standard with Cedric and frequently would become embroiled in prolonged discussions with the belligerent, irascible Maintenance Engineer who considered the instigation of the ISO quality standard to be a complete and utter waste of time. Fred had an immense hurdle to overcome in persuading Cedric to co-operate and sign up to the system.

Unfortunately Cedric had tremendous difficulty saying the word certificate, which always came out cerstificate with the superfluous S always being included in the word. Every time I talked to Fred, he invariably commented on Cedric's mispronunciation of the word, saying to me,

'Have you noticed Cedric is unable to pronounce the word "certificate"?'

'Yeah,' I replied, 'funny isn't it?'

One day after a particularly gruelling afternoon in the company of Cedric arguing about the Quality system and the cerstificates. Fred suddenly realised he too had picked up Cedric's idiosyncrasies, discovering much to his consternation he too kept saying the word certificates. He later judged it best to keep out of Cedric's way in order not to become permanently contaminated with this mispronunciation of the word.

It was totally bizarre, as Cedric appeared to know how the word should be pronounced, yet, unable to correctly say the word himself, not realising his incorrect pronunciation. I once said the word as certificates repeatedly to him just to observe the response. Richard happened to be in the laboratory when I did this. He knew of Cedric's difficulty in saying the word and fully aware I was winding up the maintenance engineer. After I had said the word certificate a number of times, Cedric, in his usual charming, ingratiating manner, asked me to repeat the word, which I did.

'Certificate,' I repeated, ensuring the incorrect pronunciation was clearly stated.

'Why you ignorant, stupid bastard, you can't even say the word properly!' he informed me in his inimitable, ingratiating, charming, people friendly manner. I looked at Richard, giving him a secret smile concerning the statement just made by the Maintenance Engineer. Richard just shook his head in disbelief, fully aware how we wound each other up.

I believe to this day, Cedric still says Certificates, but I suppose Fred now says it as it should be pronounced managing to shake off Cedric's contaminating effect. Unfortunately towards the end of 1991, Fred was made redundant from Hyperwaste, by Tom Driscoll, primarily because Fred had been a close friend of Dave Parry, the former Managing Director and any friend of Dave, was no friend of Tom's.

I felt sorry to see Fred leave but there would be a lot more upheavals during my time at Hyperwaste before I too eventually left.

CHAPTER 4

*W*ithout a doubt, working for Hyperwaste, particularly during the early days at the old refinery, certainly falls into another happy period of my life, recalled with fondness. Memories of working alongside characters such as Jamie Soames, Cedric Hughes, Helen Jones, Richard Cooper, and Fred Germaine, it is another happy compartment of my rather eclectic life.

Following orders from the local council, Hyperwaste ceased taking in waste materials and after a few more weeks, the WDA also prohibited the company from treating any of the unprocessed waste remaining on the site, all at the insistence of their paymasters, the Council which at that time they reported to. The overall local Council, included some Councillors of extremely dubious, hypocritical character.

During one of my nights out in the neighbouring valley and the town and where Repeat Controls, one of my previous employers had a large facility. Consequently, I knew quite a number of people. This particular evening, I bumped into Paul who worked for the Waste Disposal Authority department of the Council. He had consumed quite a few intoxicating drinks that night making him less inhibited and more vocal than normal, instilling him with the confidence he normally lacked. Often on visits to the plant, he tended to be quiet, leaving his boss Dave Evans to carry out most of the discussion. He called me aside, slurring his words due to the excessive amount of alcohol, which he had consumed and began explaining the situation to me through his alcoholic breath.

'You see Vinnie, we have nothing against Hyperwaste or you. In fact, we think the plant is a fucking good idea, it is just those bastards on the Council, they tell us what to do and we follow orders. Unfortunately, they pay our salaries. It is nothing personal. Here, let me buy you another drink!' With that, he garbled his order for two more pints of beer to the attractive barmaid of The Gwesty Bach pub.

If the Environment Agency, now an independent environmental, legislative body had existed in the late eighties, during all these problems, the plant, would in all probability, still be operational. Although it was gratifying to know the people, with the technical ability and knowledge working for the Council were actually on our side. Unfortunately they still followed instructions from their paymasters and particularly some of the unscrupulous, corrupt members.

The very early days of the plant consisted of Richard Cooper, Jamie Soames, Helen the secretary who Richard had employed, Cedric and I. Towards the latter part of 1989, Fred Germaine made his appearance on site. Fred had acquired his position due to his friendship with Dave Parry, the Managing Director of the company at the time, both belonged to the same Golf club.

By the end of the autumn 1989, the garage reached completion ready for the diesel mechanics to move in and work on the fleet of vehicles from the depot situated about thirty miles away, on the outskirts of Cardiff. Indeed the garage being large could accommodate the largest of the articulated vehicles for repair and prepare them for plating or in non-technical language MOT for large vehicles. Colin George, the chief Fitter with Alastair Lawson a tough, no nonsense, Scotsman from Glasgow as his right hand man. Both originally based near Swansea, but enticed by monetary

45

incentives to work at the treatment site. Later to be joined by Julian, the apprentice. Julian obtained the position primarily through nepotism, being the son of the Fleet Engineering Director. Two more indentured fitters, Phil and Jacob joined them who lived locally near Jamie in a small hamlet on the outskirts of Ebbw Vale. Jamie was quite friendly with both Phil and Jacob prior to their commencing work with the company.

The people working in the maintenance garage were also real characters. Phil came up to me one day and told me the story of Alastair and Julian. Alastair originated from Glasgow, possessing an extremely strong, barely understandable, Scottish accent. I must confess when he talked to me, I had great difficulty understanding him. Phil could not stop himself laughing as he related the story. Alastair or Jock as we sometimes called him, had been working in the pit on the underside of one of the vehicles. Phil kept explaining during his story how he too had difficulty in understanding Jock when he spoke and sometimes used lip reading as a way of guessing what the Scotsman had been imparting to him during their conversations. Julian had been standing above the pit when Jock shouted for him to bring something, Phil said he could not understand what Jock had said, but Julian, the apprentice went off as if he did. Shortly afterwards Julian returned with a wing mirror for one of the lorry units then passed it down to Jock. With that Jock, came out from the underside of the vehicle and immediately began ranting and raving at Julian in his broad Scottish accent.

'What the fuck is this?' he asked angrily, brandishing the wing mirror like a scimitar in front of the bemused, terrified apprentice.

'I asked yaeh for a 14 mil spanner, why the fuck did you bring me this, och cannae no understand plain, foocking English?' he shouted and once again wielding the totally superfluous wing mirror. Having vented his anger, Alastair then stormed off to get the required spanner from his toolbox.

Apart from Cedric and the minor arguments, everyone worked well as a team and there tended to be a reasonably friendly atmosphere around the site. It was *Déjà vu* for me having experienced exactly the same feelings in the old West Mercian Oil days at the very beginning, during the halcyon days of Craig Theake.

The contractors from a fabricating company were also on the site, they had acquired the contract for installing a super-duper filter press and huge reciprocating, high-pressure Willet pumps used for pumping the neutralised sludge through the press. The soluble oil treatment plant although intact from the days of West Mercian Oil required a bit of modification and maintenance, which the contractor had to do together with installing a huge clarifier used for agglomerating the sludge prior to the filtration process and installing the attendant pumps and pipe work. The clarifier was huge, with the capability of containing almost half a million gallons of liquid with a huge stirrer which slowly moved and compacted the sludge in preparation for the filtering process. Hyperwaste carried on with the installation despite the forthcoming legal battle with the local Council and the Development agency, a battle which the directors of the company felt confident in winning.

I seemed to be forever working for companies who appeared to be in the media spotlight. The whole situation between Hyperwaste and the council even had a satirical article in the magazine Private Eye, dedicated to the scenario, in which the local council appeared to come off worse, with the magazine portraying the Councillors as buffoons and idiots. Still, all this media

47

attention made life that more interesting and there tended not to be many quiet days on site, between demonstrators appearing in front of the gates at the drop of a hat, shouting waving their placards and banners closely accompanied by local politicians, television cameras and newspaper journalists.

It was about this time at the site, both Colin George and Alastair Lawson experienced a horrendous accident with one of the company vehicles. They had both been taken down to the Cardiff depot to pick up a skip lorry on which the hydraulics appeared to be malfunctioning. Both got into the vehicle and then drive it back to the treatment plant for repair. While they were travelling back to the site, the mechanics failed to notice the hydraulic arms on the skip lorry slowly rising, because of the hydraulic malfunction. En route, the vehicle had to pass under a bridge and slightly lower than the average bridge. The skip lorry, in ordinary circumstances would normally have passed under it quite easily but the skip lifting arms had risen higher than usual. When the vehicle drove under the bridge, the arm caught the underside of the structure, bringing the vehicle to an abrupt and unexpected halt.

As the vehicle jolted violently, the force caused the cab of the vehicle to tip over abruptly. The cab pivoted in this way, allowing convenient access to the engine compartment for ease of engine maintenance.

Alastair was driving the vehicle and his arm went through the steering wheel, badly damaging his shoulder, almost wrenching the arm away from its socket. Normally when one can perceive an accident is about to happen, it is possible to brace oneself, however neither Alastair nor Colin knew the accident was about to occur and the first they knew about it came about after waking up from an unconscious state and discovering themselves upside down in the flipped over cab of the vehicle.

The result of this horrendous accident meant Colin being off work for a number of weeks with whiplash and Alastair having to undergo extensive surgery on his right arm. The surgery went wrong and he nearly lost the arm after he suffered from infection in the wound following the initial operation.

Alastair never fully recovered after the completely horrific accident, never regaining complete working capability of his right arm. Being right handed meant he could not use the required force for using implements as, screwdrivers, spanners and torque wrenches etc.

The Scottish fitter went on long-term sickness, his career after the accident as a diesel mechanic at an end. Colin brought him to the plant for a visit a long time after the incident. He appeared to be upbeat about the whole incident, despite the loss of his career. The last we heard, he moved back up to Scotland with his wife and children.

CHAPTER 5

*W*ithin a few weeks of joining Hyperwaste, the plant was prohibited from accepting or even treating any of the oils already on the site. To all intents and purpose, the plant could be considered shut down due to all these restrictions now imposed upon the company by the local council. The powers that be in the higher echelons of Hyperwaste, namely Dave Moreland and Richard Mainwaring, decided the company should try to utilise my services and chemical experience more effectively and as much as possible. It was considered one of the additional duties I could perform involved picking up chemicals and taking them to disposal sites, helping the depots during the holiday periods, particularly during *the silly season* in the summer, when there tended to be an acute shortage of drivers at the depots, with many being away on vacation.

Firstly, one legal obstacle had to be overcome, every driver involved in the transportation of hazardous materials has, by law, to undergo an ADR course (*Accord European Relatif Au Transport International Des Merchandises Dangereuses par Route*). Which is quite a mouthful, hence the necessary abbreviation. Despite my chemical qualifications, the company had no wish to become embroiled in fighting another legal case involving an employee driving a vehicle loaded with toxic and hazardous chemicals without the relevant ADR qualification. Hence, the company considered it prudent to send me on an ADR course, ensuring everything was done by the book and not cause any unnecessary, additional, litigious complications. Hyperwaste had enough to contend with fighting the case in trying to obtain a waste disposal site licence for the newly acquired treatment facility, without any further unnecessary additional, easily avoidable difficulties. Everyone knew full well the action committee and council with their capabilities of jumping on any opportunity presented to them in making political and PR capital out of the company's actions which appeared not to conform to the rules in some way. Such a case would be an ideal opportunity, indicating the company had no intention of abiding by the hazardous waste regulations and giving the action committee more '*grist for the mill.*'

After attending an ADR course and successfully completing the programme, I delivered a few loads of hazardous materials to local disposal sites without any mishaps. That is until one day.

On that specific day, I received a phone call from Ryan Rhys, the Depot Manager at Cardiff. He did not have sufficient drivers to fulfil all the next day's schedule and asked if I could deliver ten drums, each containing approximately 200 litres of concentrated cyanide solution waste and transport them on a 7.5 tonne rigid taut liner to a disposal site located on the outskirts of Bristol. A taut liner is a flatbed vehicle with plastic curtains on all sides. Because I had possessed a full driving licence since the seventies, it allowed me to drive this size of vehicle without having to undergo an additional driving test, what is known as '*grandfather's rights*'. So this posed no problem. After conferring with Richard Cooper he agreed I could do the requested collection the next day, with things being fairly quiet at the treatment plant.

The waste cyanide solution had to be collected from a customer's facility in Cardiff, and then delivered to the treatment plant on the outskirts of Bristol. Unfortunately the waste could not be collected until just before lunchtime, but still allowing sufficient time to collect the waste, deliver the ten drums to the disposal site, then return the empty 7.5 tonne vehicle to the depot for later collection by the hire company.

I drove the company pool car to the depot at Cardiff where the hire vehicle had been left. After arriving at the depot, I indulged in some idle chit chat with Ryan and the girls in the office before collecting the relevant the paperwork, tremcard, hazchem boards and the 'section17' paperwork. The 'section 17' or pre-notification paperwork for the shipment of hazardous waste was a legal requirement when transporting hazardous waste. It contained all the information as to the type of waste, its concentration and where the waste originated and final destination. It also contained the name of the properly authorised waste carrier and the name of the disposal site, ensuring it was equipped and licenced to either store, or treat the particular waste being shipped there. The section 17 contained quite a few copy pages, each to be kept by the various companies involved in the operation and a copy for each of the relevant Waste Disposal authorities, the WDA for the disposal site, and one for the WDA for the source, the customer. All the copies to be signed by the parties involved. After collecting all the necessary documentation and cyanide antidote kit, I left to collect the waste from the customer's site at Caerphilly.

Now, I am not the best driver in the world and driving a large 7.5 tonne vehicle caused me some worry and consternation. Because of this apprehension, I drove the vehicle fairly sedately, whilst making my way along the highways and by-ways to the customer's site, without any problem but extremely nervous, unaccustomed to driving such a hefty sized vehicle.

At the collection site, the ten plastic, bung top drums, each containing approximately 200 litres of the concentrated cyanide solution were loaded onto the flatbed of the taut liner without any problems. After getting the paperwork signed by the authorised person at the British Airways maintenance works, I made my way up the M4 heading east-bound on the carriageway towards the allocated disposal site on the outskirts of Bristol.

By this time, it was about late lunchtime, but still sufficient time to drop the waste off before the disposal site closed for the day giving me a reasonable finishing time.

It was a nice sunny day yet, despite this fine weather, not too much traffic appeared to be on the motorway for that time of day. This was prior to the new Severn Bridge crossing, later constructed to relieve the traffic congestion on the original, initial cantilever box bridge. It was the original, Severn Bridge which I had to cross.

The taut liner appeared to be going well, however as it approached an incline on the M4 motorway, near the small hamlet called Crick, it began to losing momentum because of the rise. I pressed my foot on the accelerator giving more power to the struggling vehicle. Nothing happened, the vehicle did not speed up. Once more, I pressed harder on the accelerator pedal, still the tachometer did not budge, if anything it decreased in speed. I changed down the gears, but the vehicle still slowed down. I could see the tachometer still dropping, indicating the vehicle was losing vital revs and power. Evidently, there appeared to be some issue with the accelerator. If it had been the clutch, then the revs would have shot up when I pressed the accelerator pedal but the vehicle not increase in speed. This was not the case, the rev counter did not increase, ergo the accelerator was at fault in some way. The slope in the road was long and steady. There was no alternative but pull over onto the hard shoulder, otherwise the vehicle would come to a halt in the slow lane and cause all sorts of disruption to the traffic heading eastbound towards the old Severn crossing.

Unfortunately, at this time, I did not have the use of a company mobile phone, or even a personal mobile phone, and unable to contact Ryan, informing him of my predicament. After pulling the vehicle over onto the hard shoulder of the motorway, I clambered over the side of the motorway with the intention of making my way towards Crick on the A48, the Caerwent road, where hopefully, I would be able to find a telephone kiosk in full working order and which had not been vandalised by the local teenagers. After walking back to the barrier, indicating a bridge over the motorway, I scaled the barrier, before sliding down the steep embankment to the bottom alongside which passed an A class road. Which way to head, north or south? I took a gamble and headed north with the hope of finding the nearest telephone phone kiosk in that particular compass direction.

As stated, it materialized into a hot sunny day, not the sort of conditions for a brisk canter of about a mile. At last, I came upon a telephone kiosk which, thankfully, had not been vandalised.

After placing a reverse charge call to the depot at Cardiff, Sheila Clark, the office Manageress answered. Firstly, explaining my predicament to her, before speaking to Ryan. He came to the phone giving me an abrupt retort, the panic obvious in his voice after gleaning the problem from Sheila's telephone conversation.

'What have you done now. You haven't damaged the vehicle have you?' Indicating, he considered the mechanical malfunction to be my fault in some way.

'No,' I replied, indignantly, 'I think the accelerator cable has snapped.'

'Where is the vehicle now?' he asked.

I informed him it was parked on the hard shoulder of the M4.

'Right,' he replied, 'I'll get onto the hire company and ask them to send a fitter out to you. Meanwhile get back to the vehicle and wait there until he arrives.'

After returning to the truck, I sat in the cab, contentedly listening to the music on the radio and waited to be rescued.

Almost two hours later, a repair vehicle pulled up behind me on the hard shoulder and a mechanic got out. I explained the problem to him as best I could, and impart my amateur opinion as to the source of the fault. The mechanic flipped the cab open, inspecting the engine before confirming my suspicion. Indeed, the throttle cable had snapped. Vehicles whizzed at speed past the stricken taut liner while the mechanic investigated the problem.

'I'm going to have to ask a big favour of you,' he began, before continuing.

'I can't work here with the traffic going past like this. However, I can do a temporary patch up job which will get you up the road and where you can get off they motorway at the Chepstow junction. There is a large lay-by where I can do a better job on the vehicle. The only problem is the temporary job will mean the accelerator will be at full throttle, which also means you will be hurtling up the road at speed and you will have to stop almost immediately in the lay-by and then immediately go into neutral. Do you think you can do that?'

My mouth went dry after the mechanic explained the forthcoming scenario to me. Wishing not to appear a wimp, I replied with dried lips nearly glued together because of the parchedness being experienced.

'Yeah, sure. No sweat.' A complete lie, on all counts, especially the sweat part. I had no idea whether or not I could indeed do it. This day was the first time I had experienced driving a large 7.5 tonne truck and the thought of driving it at speed with almost 2,000 litres of concentrated cyanide solution on board was not my idea of a practice run.

The mechanic continued. 'Right let's get started then!' With that, he tinkered for a while with the accelerator cable, then shortly afterwards, proclaimed victoriously.

'That should do it. Are you ready?'

'Ok,' I replied not certain if I was indeed ready or not.

The mechanic flipped the cab back down into the position, clamped it down before starting the engine. The engine sounded as if it was in agony, screaming at high pitch, with the higher than normal revolutions. It sounded, to all intents, as if it were a creature being tortured.

The mechanic got out of the cab and shouted his instructions while we were at the nearside of the vehicle to be heard over the whine of the truck and the motorway traffic hurtling by the vehicle.

'Right, I must warn you when you let out the clutch, the vehicle will shoot up the road, as the throttle is set to fast as you can hear from the scream of the engine. Try to get into the lay-by on the left at the Chepstow junction. Are we ready to go?'

'As Ready as I will ever be,' I answered, then adding, 'let's do it'

The mechanic replied, 'I'll follow you.' Getting into the screaming vehicle, I began positioning myself as comfortable as possible. The mechanic got into his vehicle, after he had firmly ensconced himself in the maintenance vehicle, I waited for a large break in the traffic, pressed the clutch down flat to the floor and put the gear stick into first gear. Letting the clutch out slowly, whilst releasing the handbrake, the vehicle shot forward at a great rate of knots, like a greyhound shooting out of a starting box.

Upon entering the slow lane of the M4 the vehicle hurtled forward, with the engine still screaming due to the high revolutions being forced upon it. The perspiration was running down my back, saturating my shirt. Both my palms were sweaty and clammy, my heart pounded and my mouth still bone dry. Here I was driving a 7.5 tonne, high-sided vehicle at high speed with almost 2 tonnes of highly concentrated cyanide solution on board. Not my idea of calm, relaxing day. The vehicle hurtled along the motorway while my eyes remained firmly glued upon the road ahead.

This was the relatively easy part. My mind jumped ahead to the Chepstow junction and the lay-by. *'Please, please God let there be no vehicles in the lay-by.'* I am not a religious person, but any help when up against it.

Suddenly the sign post for junction and the Chepstow turn off appeared … oh God! I indicated my intention to turn up the slip road and climbed the incline.

'Please, please let there be no traffic appearing from my right on the roundabout.' From my elevated position in the cab, it became evident there were no other vehicles on the roundabout.

'Praise be the lord!'

Luck was with me, no traffic on the roundabout meant not having to stop with an engine at high revs. I didn't even change down, and couldn't, even if I wanted to as the lower gears could not cope with the high revolutions of the engine.

The vehicle hurtled onto the roundabout road and I turned the steering wheel left, not too viciously, otherwise the vehicle might overturn and I did not want a major incident with over 2,000 litres of concentrated cyanide solution lying in pools all over the tarmac.

Steering the vehicle safely onto the Chepstow road, I could see in the distance, there were no vehicles parked in the lay-by ahead. I could not believe it, my luck was still holding.

Once again, indicating left, I steered the vehicle into the lay-by still at high speed. The instant the vehicle was in the lay by, I put the gear stick into neutral and braked, not too harshly so as not to send myself plunging through the windscreen or the drums of concentrated cyanide solution careering in the back of the vehicle.

The 7.5 tonne truck came to a halt. I put on the handbrake and turned off the agonizing scream of the engine. By this time I was perspiring with fear, my shirt absolutely sodden. Resting my head on my forearms on the steering wheel. I waited for the mechanic to arrive, appreciating the silence, now that the sound of the screaming engine had stopped, I wallowed in the anti-climax after the excitement and my fear quickly evaporated.

Within a short period of time, the mechanic appeared at the side of the vehicle and opened the cab door.

'Well done,' he said exhibiting a broad smile on his face. 'That was impressive driving.' With that I got out of the cab and he started working on the throttle cable.

'How long do you think you will be?' I asked.

'About an hour,' he replied.

There was a phone box nearby and so I made a phone call to the depot. By now it was 3:30 pm to tell them the news so far and ask what they wanted me to do. Ryan came onto the Phone and when I explained the situation, he replied

'It's too late to go to the Disposal site now. I will phone and tell them. You make your way back to the depot park up the vehicle and one of the drivers will take the load to the disposal site first thing in the morning.'

I was not too upset at the instructions. After an hour as promised, the mechanic repaired the broken throttle cable, but this time the vehicle did not whine as if in pain when he started it up.

With that I thanked him and headed back to the depot.

Mercifully, that was the only hair-rising experience I ever had while carrying toxic waste.

CHAPTER 6

*B*ecause of the restrictions imposed upon the company by the local council, namely, curtailing the processing of oils at the treatment facility, the company deemed that in addition to setting up the laboratory, performing chemical analysis and collecting hazardous wastes, they should also utilise my skills in other areas of Chemistry/Chemical Engineer, sending me further afield to other Hyperwaste facilities dispersed throughout the United Kingdom. These imposed, extra duties granted me the opportunity of inspecting other sites and interact with Hyperwaste personnel throughout the country, allowing me the ability to put faces to the voices I frequently conversed with over the phone. Besides, it was enjoyable travelling around the UK visiting other parts of the country, areas I would not normally consider going away to.

These trips regularly required a considerable amount of time away from home. Stella did not seem to mind, an unrealised indication of a cooling in her feelings and passions towards me. Whereas Cindy, my first wife, would not have been too pleased about the time spent away from home and insist I seek alternative employment in another field of industry, involving far less travel and enforced absence.

As far as the packaging side of hazardous chemicals was concerned, I became quite proficient in the identification, packaging, and correct labelling of wastes for transportation by road, adhering to the new waste regulations being imposed upon the waste industry and continually being modified by the EU and mandarins in the Civil Service. The statutory regulations periodically tightened and the goal posts narrowed due to the abuse rife in the industry involving some of the smaller waste disposal companies, specifically when it came to the disposal of hazardous materials.

Malcolm Roundtree, my mentor, during those weeks prior to working on the project in Carlisle taught me a considerable amount, bringing me up to speed concerning the packaging of hazardous chemicals, ensuring complete conformity to the newly imposed regulations, making certain I was fully conversant with the laws regarding the labelling of the miscellaneous wastes.

Hyperwaste also had an excellent reputation in the field of chemical cleaning operations, which basically required the flushing, cleaning and sometimes passivating (chemical protection) of chemical storage or process vessels with their connecting pipe-work, using a plethora of chemicals, depending upon the requirements. A Chemist was usually required to do the chemical analysis to ensure the chemicals being used had the correct concentrations, also any neutralisation required, was properly and safely adhered to. Instead of hiring a local Industrial Chemist, the bean counters (accountants) considered it more financially beneficial to use my technical knowledge and expertise, with the added bonus of the services being provided cheaply. Richard Cooper did not charge the other divisions an exorbitant fee for my services and time. Thus, with the costs being maintained in-house, inexpensive and not profiting other companies, I began discovering myself in great demand throughout the UK, not because of my technical ability, but purely because of these cut-price deals on offer by my boss. He had become a pimp, prostituting my services.

My first meeting with the managers from the Middlesborough Depot came about during a pre-tender meeting, which the Chemical Cleaning Team was trying to put together for Conoco at Immingham located on the banks of the Humber Estuary. The supervisors from Middlesborough had requested me to be in attendance during the initial meeting as they intended employing my services as the resident Chemist during the term of the project. It was potentially a huge venture with the promise of large amounts of money to be made for the company. The isomerisation plant, for that particular section of the oil refinery, had not been cleaned since its inception some five years earlier.

The isomerisation process replaced the older, environmentally detrimental process of adding tetraethyl lead (TEM) used for the elimination of 'knocking' in petrol engines. Unfortunately, TEM emitted high concentrations of lead into the atmosphere from the engine exhausts and because of these environmental considerations, TEM became prohibited and completely phased out, with lead free petrol ultimately becoming the only petrol available at the petrol stations. Manufacturing of this more environmentally friendly, lead free fuel required a highly sophisticated isomerisation process in the oil refineries. Because of its time in use, the isomerisation operation at Humberside required cleaning due to excessive build-up of solids within the extensive pipe-work and process equipment. The resultant chemical cleaning operation would be quite a large undertaking, requiring installing huge lagoons to take the millions of gallons of cleaning chemicals generated during the operation.

It was during this meeting, I first came across John Andrews the Depot Manager and John Willis, the

Chemical Cleaning Manager, enjoying their company immensely, both no-nonsense, straight talking northerners, very practical, 'hands on' type of guys. To assess the enormity of the project, we all had to venture into parts of the refinery where engineers rarely went, necessitating us attiring in full chemical protection suits, due to the possibility of hydrofluoric acid (HF) leaks used in the isomerisation refining operation. The new Plant Engineer had not even been out on site, so it was a new experience for him too, with all the processing of the unleaded petrol being managed from the main control room via circuits and computers.

John Willis, the project manager was not happy at the prospect of working with Hydrofluoric acid and venturing out into parts of the refinery deemed to be highly dangerous mainly because of the chemical. As it transpired, Hyperwaste did not win the contract, primarily based on price. However, it was because of this initial meeting with the two Johns, they requested my help on other chemical cleaning projects whenever a chemist was required on site by their clients.

An opportunity first presented itself within a few weeks of getting involved in the aforementioned chemical cleaning operation, when a chemical company based in Hartlepool required passivating of some new stainless steel tanks and attendant pipe-work and specified the testing of for the removal of iron by a piece of equipment known as Atomic absorption spectra photometer. The very piece of equipment we had at the treatment plant in South Wales, able to analyse for iron and any other metals down to concentrations of ppm (parts per million).

I journeyed to Hartlepool with the Atomic Absorption Spectrophotometer securely stashed in the rear of the hired Vauxhall estate car. Hartlepool and Middlesborough are located quite close to each other.

63

So the Hyperwaste arranged the accommodation billeting me in a local hotel, the Billingham arms, for the duration of the project.

By this time, I had become well-acquainted with John Willis, discovering he enjoyed ingesting alcoholic beverages, particularly beer. While at the depot and the first night of my stay at the Billingham Arms, John informed me in his broad North East accent.

'Whey man, it's not worth me going home this early as the traffic is too heavy around Stockton-on-Tees, I'll come to the hotel with you and have a couple of pints, just to keep you company for an hour or so like.'

The two of us arrived at the Hotel at about six pm, arriving in our separate company vehicles, almost immediately making our way to the hotel bar. As I was on expenses John told me to get the drinks in and also get him a cigar while I was at it. Upon observing my quizzical expression he began explaining,

'Whey up man, don't worry It's all coming out of my budget. As Richard Cooper is charging me for your time and expenses, all I have to do is pass the invoice.'

After about half an hour or so, John requested more beer and so the evening progressed in this fashion. Meanwhile we discussed Hyperwaste and a plethora of other topics such as his time with the company, the office politics and the attractive girls working there and such like. We also discussed our personal lives and partners, in addition to sorting out the world's problems. Interspersed with these conversations, I kept going to the bar to get more alcoholic beverages, John managing to consume two drinks compared to my one. By about 10:45, John experienced some difficulty in focusing his extremely bloodshot eyes on the timepiece strapped to his left wrist. Casually and slurring his words in his north-eastern accent.

'I suppose I had better phone the mishus to come and get me and leave my car here.' With that he staggered to the pay phone to contact his long suffering wife. After a short while he returned.

'How did she take it?' I enquired.

'She's alright, she knows me too well,' he replied, before adding,

'I think I'll have a whisky before I go.' Once more, for the umpteenth time that evening, I obediently returned to the bar putting the cost of yet another drink on the ever increasing bar tab.

John left the bar at about 11:10 and went to his spouse sitting in the family car, probably quietly fuming while she waited for him to appear.

From that time onwards, during the remainder of that particular project and whenever I went to Billingham, this ritual tended to be repeated. Upon being informed of an impending visit by me and staying at the Billingham arms. John's long suffering wife would casually remark.

'I guess it will be another late night for you then and you will probably need yet another lift?'

On one occasion on receiving the bill for my services, John Andrews, the depot manager phoned Richard Cooper informing him in jest, he would be deducting at least £100 for the bar bill as I had been drinking with John Willis and putting it on the expenses and he was not willing to foot the excessive amount.

I enjoyed my visits to Cleveland immensely, finding the people from Teesside friendly, funny and helpful. What did surprise me was the animosity which existed between people from Teesside and Tyneside, erroneously believing Tyneside and Teesside to be classified as the same area. Not a bit of it, they are totally different locations, the accents may be similar but they have different attitudes, with each area exhibiting an intense dislike towards the other. A similar antipathy exists today in South Wales between the indigenous populations of Swansea and Cardiff.

My presence had also been requested on a chemical cleaning operation at for a big multinational company based in Newcastle. John wanted me to supervise the whole operation. Laboratory experiments previously carried out by me on the material contaminating two huge tanks indicated cleaning with organic solvent would be more efficacious than the usual sulphamic acid. John Willis would quite happily work with any acid or alkali, however when it came to working with organic flammable solvents, he tended to be wary because of the flammability and flash point i.e. the temperature at which the solvent is able to ignite. I would have liked to recommend a fairly strong solvent such as Methyl Ethyl Ketone for the process with a flash point of minus 9 Degrees Celsius. However, as a compromise, I eventually agreed to use Iso Propyl Alcohol with a more reasonable flash point of plus 12 Degrees Celsius. Being so cold up in Tyneside, that temperature would not be reached, especially with the project taking place during February. The whole process involved setting up equipment consisting of rotating jets and extensive pipe work requiring intrinsically safe electrical equipment and pumps. The project was to be carried out for a large chemical manufacturer based in Jarrow on the outskirts of Newcastle, necessitating an hour journey from Billingham. I thought I would stay in Newcastle, with John away on vacation and to save on travelling time, allowing me a longer stay in bed before breakfasting. That idea was shattered when the team from Billingham kept telling me what rough places Newcastle and Jarrow were and how you could not look at a Geordie without some sort of aggression on their part. In addition, the team would not talk to the workforce at the customer's site. It was always left up to me when borrowing equipment or asking for help. Contrary to the team's opinions, I found the Geordies very helpful and believe the guys from Teesside were just being paranoid. Their paranoia did, however, put the fear of God into me about staying in Newcastle for the duration of the project, particularly the first day a Thursday.

'Way up man, it's Thursday night and pay night and there's bound to be trouble in town man with them out on the piss like. You're liable to get stabbed or mugged. Man, it's a real rough area.'

Being a pacifist and devout coward, I travelled back down to Teesside that night, once again booking myself into the familiar Billingham Hotel for the next few days during the forecast period of the project. I believe the guys from Middlesbrough over-reacted because I found the Geordie workforce extremely helpful and co-operative and, contrary to my information, very friendly. We would not have completed the job as quickly as we did without their assistance.

One project carried out for the Teesside depot nearly resulted in disastrous consequences for Hyperwaste, while working for a large company near Seal Sands on the outskirts of Hartlepool which required a chemical cleaning operation performed on a couple of their counter current, tube heat exchangers. The Middleborough plant had done this operation on numerous occasions, using a chemical called Sulphamic acid. However this time was different. There was a new high flying Project Engineer who had recently joined the company and wanted to make a name for himself. He had attended a seminar where it had been recommended a weak solution of

Hydrofluoric acid be used as the cleaning acid for mild steel instead of the relatively mild sulphamic acid.

John Willis, had years of experience in the chemical cleaning operation behind him, arguing vehemently together with the customer's Process Engineer against the use of hydrofluoric acid as the main cleaning agent. Although not present at the meeting, I agreed wholeheartedly with John, Hydrofluoric acid is highly corrosive towards most metals, including stainless steel. These huge exchangers were made of mild steel which is even more susceptible to attack by the aggressive acid, But not only that, Hydrofluoric acid is also an extremely dangerous acid with the ability to permeate through skin and attack the bone marrow with the possibility of causing leukaemia and other cancers. When using Hydrofluoric acid, a special gel has to be carried Calcium Gluconate which is the only agent which counteracts the effect of the acid on skin.

Despite John's and the Process Engineer's protestations against the use of Hydrofluoric acid, the Project Engineer had his way with the client's higher management choosing to use Hydrofluoric acid as the cleaning agent following his advice.

John was on vacation during the operation, and his deputy Malcolm Jones, left in charge. My presence was only asked for at the operation to help with the analysis. The operation went well and we completed the operation on the Sunday ready for the production start up the following Monday morning.

I finished late on the Sunday evening, organising disposal of the spent hydrofluoric acid and ensuring the correct tanker was used with a rubber lining. I had a quiet evening in the hotel with John being away and not ingesting too much alcohol.

The next morning, before wending my way south heading back to South Wales, I thought I would first call in to the Depot offices imparting my farewells before taking to the road. On my way through the small building, I bumped into John Andrews whom I perceived had an extremely worried look on his face, exhibiting a high state of agitation.

'Vinson, can I have a word with you in my office?' No hint of a smile on his face. We both went into his office and he shut the door behind us, never a good sign. He continued, 'I just had a phone call from the customer, it appears the heat exchangers are leaking and product is going into the hot water system and vice versa, the product is contaminating the water. It looks as if the hydrofluoric acid has attacked the heat exchanger tubes, causing the leaks. They have had to suspend production to resolve the problem. I just hope we do not get the blame for this. Were there any problems and did everything go okay, basically have we cocked up?' He was extremely forthright in his questioning.

I assured him we had done everything as instructed and maintained the acid strength as stipulated in the quite extensive method statement, with all analysis results, times etc. thoroughly documented.

'God, I wish John Willis was here,' he stated, with more than a hint of desperation in his voice.

'Will you come with me to visit the site so we can have a chat with the Process Engineer?' Reluctantly, I agreed, although with no wish in being berated by an irate engineer and the future possibility of being involved in legal action against our company possibly amounting to hundreds of thousands of pounds or even running into millions, but I could not leave John to face the music alone.

John drove me to the customer's facility in his car. Once on site we both made our way to the control room where the Process Engineer could usually be found, like the captain of a great sea going vessel. He was not the engineer who had insisted on using hydrofluoric acid that particular responsibility and decision lay with the young, ambitious Project Engineer.

I had met the Process Engineer on a couple of occasions before and during the operation. In his fifties, with grey hair and a vast amount of chemical experience, he appeared to be a reasonable guy, but I knew full well his demeanour could alter dramatically after having received a bollocking and thorough *arse reaming* from his superiors.

Both John and I approached him with trepidation, fully expecting an abusive tirade about the damage which his precious equipment had sustained during the chemical cleaning operation. Being a former Process Engineer myself during previous incarnations, I was fully aware how protective we (Process Engineers) can be towards our process equipment, bordering on almost paternalistic and obsessive, similar to someone who looks after a classic car, continually cleaning and maintaining the equipment. We hesitantly, looked at the Process Engineer, not knowing what to say for fear of incriminating ourselves and the company.

'Good morning,' he said, no hint of anger or recrimination towards us, either in his voice or in his general demeanour. In fact he appeared surprisingly cheerful considering his plant had been 'fucked up' using the correct technical, Chemical Engineering jargon.

'How bad is it?' enquired John tentatively, not wishing to say too much, fearing implicating Hyperwaste in some way and ultimately incurring huge litigious action against the company. To our complete and utter astonishment, the Process Engineer went into a calm, long speech about his beloved process equipment.

'The two main process heat exchangers are fucked, but don't worry about it, it's not Hyperwaste's fault. I told that jumped up Project Engineer not to use hydrofluoric acid and so did John Willis, but, no, he had to have his own way and insisted on using Hydrofluoric acid. HF is okay with new systems, but these exchangers have been in use over 25 years and basically on their last legs. The HF finally finished them off. Your company adhered to procedures to the letter. I have checked all the figures and analysis. Your company has done nothing wrong and are completely exonerated.'

I spoke slightly hesitantly, 'Well, if you don't mind me saying, you don't seem too upset about it?'

'I've been asking for two new heat exchangers for years, that Project Engineer has actually done me a favour and he gets the blame for it, so we are all covered. I wanted to use sulphamic acid as did John Willis. It's all in writing and our reports are to that effect and stating the possible outcome by using HF, which is exactly what has transpired. So don't worry about it, I'm not.'

Both John and I stayed for a while indulging in small talk with the Engineer, trying not to look too relieved at this unexpected outcome at not being implicated in this process catastrophe.

We made our way to John's car where we sat and had a talk for a while.

'I should have known John Willis would have covered our arses should anything go wrong, he's been in the business too many years to be caught out.' John pontificated, the relief obvious in his face, also exhibiting unbridled admiration for his subordinate.

'So we're off the hook,' he added.

'There's obviously not much love between those two engineers,' I replied before adding 'Thank God.'

71

'Too true!' agreed John. After a brief discourse John Andrews finally started his car and we headed back to the depot where I had left my company car.

'There's no need for you to stay Vinson,' John added. 'You may as well head home, if there is a problem you may have to come back up. Although, I don't think there will be any form of witch hunt as far as Hyperwaste is concerned. Thanks for coming with me to the plant.'

'I didn't do anything,' I replied,

'No, it was just nice to have the morale support. I just didn't fancy going into the lion's den alone.'

That morning I headed back to South Wales with a seven hour journey ahead of me, somewhat relieved at the outcome, considering how our meeting could have turned out, with the possibility of a slanging match. I turned on the radio listened to the music at full blast, enjoying the nice sunny weather and a leisurely, solitary drive heading back to South Wales and Stella, ah bliss.

John Willis later informed me there had been heated discussions prior to the project in which the experienced Process Engineer argued vehemently against using HF as the cleaning agent. He had been overruled by Manufacturing Manager and Plant Director, both preferring to listen to the young Project Manager's council, who was supposed to be the up and coming whiz kid. Both John and the Process Engineer had put their objections in writing as well as arguing the case verbally.

So when the whole project turned out as they prognosticated, the Process Engineer was upbeat, hence the reason for his good nature during our visit following the calamity.

There's nothing quite as uplifting as being completely vindicated in ones belief and predictions and that is exactly how the Process Engineer felt.

CHAPTER 7

*H*yperwaste came into existence after a number of waste disposal and industrial chemical cleaning companies merged to form a much larger corporation concurrent with the prevailing idea of business at the time, 'Big is beautiful.' However these numerous mergers resulted in a large amount of directors and managers being generated. Because of this, during the early days of its inception, Hyperwaste experienced tremendous financial difficulties, primarily because of being extremely top heavy at higher management level with all these miscellaneous company directors and an excess of management personnel, all being paid rather exorbitant salaries, exacerbated by all the other concomitant perks, top of the range company cars, unrestricted expense accounts, the new, innovative, expensive mobile phones, relatively new laptops, and all sorts of electronic gismos which were then just making an appearance, all part of the yuppie culture of the eighties and subsequent decades. At that time, any yuppie worth his salt had to have all these developing electronic accessories. All these aforementioned perks added to the creaking and buckling financial edifice which was Hyperwaste.

During the early days of the merger, the company directors endeavoured desperately to remain autonomous and independent, from any large predatory conglomerates. However maintaining this stance became increasingly impossible as the company became more and more insolvent, continually running into the red and unable to pay its creditors. Finally succumbing to the inevitable and in an attempt to stave off bankruptcy and continue operating, the company sold 25 % of its shares to a French Waste Disposal Company called UPA, which, itself was a subsidiary of a giant French multinational conglomerate called Regime De L'Aqua. This influx of money from the share deal helped for a short period of time, but once again, and relatively quickly, expenditure still massively outstripped income.

Striking yet another deal, this time, increasing the stake held by UPA to 48%. Not quite overall majority of the company, but nevertheless quite substantial and enough of a holding for UPA to begin influencing the business direction which the company now took. This further acquisition of shares helped the struggling company for a while, with UPA paying off all outstanding bills. This moment of respite was only transient, for within a very short period of time, yet again, the company went into the red. By the time I joined the payroll, unbeknownst to me, Hyperwaste was in dire financial difficulties.

The company required yet more infusion of money to survive, the directors, once again with cap in hand, approached UPA for additional funding. However, and quite understandably, UPA had reached the end of their tether. In fairness, they had pumped a tremendous amount of money into the company which now began to appear like a lame duck and over which they had no overall financial control and really nothing to show for their investment. In the end there was no option, and UPA insisted on taking over complete control of the company, eventually settling for 95% of the shares with the remaining 5% being retained by some of the former directors. It was a *fête accomple*.

The French company then put in charge a Managing Director of their choosing, Tom Driscoll who had previously been on the board of directors of a major waste disposal company and competitor. He was extremely ambitious but very knowledgeable about the waste disposal industry. Dave Parry, the original Hyperwaste Managing director was paid off, it was thought his association and friendship with the Samuel Abbott the chairman could prove an embarrassment and would jeopardise setting up the first treatment plant at the original WMO site. UPA also quickly paid off the Chairman Samuel Abbott who the French multinational considered to be a complete hindrance and a total PR disaster, after being endowed with his media label of *'the toxic playboy'* by the press. Following the media fiasco with Samuel Abbott, the French Multinational decided to make the position of chairman completely redundant, installing, Tom Driscoll as CEO and in complete control of the UK Company, reporting directly to the board of UPA.

Another phase in Tom Driscoll's personal master plan involved employing former colleagues and acolytes from his former company. One by one, he began installing his former associates in prominent posts and one by one the incumbent Managers were either pushed out or sacked. As far as my position was concerned, being new to the company and so low down the ladder with a somewhat meagre income and not part of the upper management clique, I had no difficulty in surviving the management purges and being the only qualified chemical engineer in the company helped. It was all quite interesting and edifying observing all the politics from an objective viewpoint.

After the company dismissed Dave Parry, the former Managing Director and Samuel Abbott, the Chairman, Tom Driscoll continued the policy with even more sackings, beginning with the person who interviewed me, Richard Mainwaring. Richard was an interesting character very knowledgeable about the industry but a complete bull-shitter, a sort of Jeffrey Archer of the Waste Industry, informing everyone he had gained his Chemistry qualifications at Cambridge, which, although technically true, masked the true facts. Richard omitted to inform people his qualification was a HNC, not a Degree and which he obtained at Cambridge Polytechnic, not one of the well-known prestigious colleagues, another fact which he also omitted.

Still Richard was not too worried about losing his job, having been born with a silver spoon in his mouth and the recipient of a rather sizeable inheritance. The waste industry was, as it appeared to me and many others, just a hobby to Mr Mainwaring. Having made these statements, I did quite like Richard and we had a good rapport. Richard's downfall was the acrimonious personality conflict between him and Tom Driscoll. They had previously met years earlier during their early years working in the waste industry. During that time their disliking for each other gestated. By the time Tom Driscoll joined Hyperwaste as Chief Executive officer, each nurtured an intense detestation for each other, hence the reason for Richard's rather quick departure, Tom Driscoll outranking him somewhat with the heavier clout. Also, Richard no longer had the backing of his old friends, Dave Parry and Samuel Abbott, both having since departed.

One of the first of Tom's acolytes to whom I was introduced was a person called Dave Pearce, who had allegedly left his former company under a cloud, something to do with embezzlement and fraud, or so the rumours went. As I recall, these rumours were mostly perpetrated by Richard Mainwaring, who also hated Dave Pearce intensely, because of his association with the new Managing Director. This was your typical board room power struggle. There could only be one

77

winner, Tom Driscoll with his backing coming directly from the French Directors of UPA and Regime De L'Aqua the obvious favourite to come out on top.

Dave was introduced as a consultant. This was in the early days before it became apparent Tom Driscoll intended having a management purge and ruthlessly getting rid of managerial personnel. Other people appeared to treat Dave Pearce with some disdain and in truth, relatively rude to him. I am by nature a garrulous person and quite chatty and so had no hesitation when introduced to John getting involved in conversation with him. I will talk to anybody, believing I am no better than anyone, conversely, no person should lord it over me. I gave Dave the shilling tour of the small laboratory and the treatment plant. Dave was very knowledgeable about the industry and the analytical equipment, the treatment plant and equipment required for the disposing of waste chemicals safely. We hit it off, however the personnel who treated him with some disdain later regretted they behaviour towards him when, some months later Dave Pearce became Area Director, replacing Dave Moreland after he too had been sacked. Dave Pearce began immediately dismissing previously belligerent personnel or giving them a rough time, forcing them to leave of their own volition. It quickly became evident Dave Pearce was Tom Driscoll's hatchet man, doing all his dirty work.

Dave Moreland tended to be his own worst enemy. Firstly he drove around in a Porsche, which Tom Driscoll thought was not the sort of flashy ostentatious car a Director of a company should be driving around in, continually telling him he should be driving around in a Lexus or Granada or something similar which appeared more in keeping with the position of a company director.

Dave was also what could be called wide boy, utterly streetwise and one hell of a womaniser, as was proved with his flirting with Jane O' Brien the Chief Reporter from the local newspaper. He had in fact left his wife to live in Tamworth with a woman who was advising Hyperwaste on the Environmental litigation between itself and the local Council. He was hard to dislike and can only be described as a loveable rogue, an Arthur Daly type character.

Tom Driscoll's Secretary, Stephanie Smith, being the MD's PA, talked down everyone in a condescending to patronizing manner. Stephanie was a secretary, but as the MD's secretary, she considered herself to be high up within the hierarchy and pecking order, behaving accordingly. One particular day, Stephanie phoned the treatment plant and I answered the phone. Stephanie demanded to know where Dave Moreland could be found as Tom Driscoll wished to talk with him urgently. Now firstly, Dave Moreland was not at the treatment facility, secondly there was absolutely no reason why a director should inform one of his underlings as to his whereabouts for the day, a fact which I imparted to Miss Smith, however, I am convinced she thought I was covering for him, which was absolutely not the case. It shortly became common knowledge Dave Moreland was having an affair. Not long afterwards Dave Moreland left having been forced out, with Dave Pearce filling his position as Area Sales Director.

It became thoroughly intriguing watching all this political in-fighting at the top and fascinating to observe from the side-lines. I felt sorry for Richard Cooper who was hard working and conscientious and formerly Dave Moreland's right hand man, he had been promoted from plant manager to UK Waste Manager as the waste Treatment plant was on stop due to the instructions of the Local Waste Disposal authorities. During the one year he clocked up a phenomenal 70,000 miles in his new Audi. Fortunately, the new Area Director also saw what an asset he was to the company and kept him on. Although hard-working, ambitious and a company man, Richard Cooper had the rare incongruous attribute for one so ambitious of being a decent bloke.

For my part, I considered all this upheaval and uncertainty just an unfortunate part of my career destiny accepting it with a certain resigned stoicism. It did mean I travelled the country helping with technical waste disposal problems and sorting wastes for shipment also, getting involved with other aspects of the Hyperwaste operations such as the Chemical Cleaning, which was yet another string to my bow and something new and interesting. I also became more involved with the new Environmental Legislation generated by the EU. The work was extremely interesting and enjoyable. I gradually became the Technical Adviser for Hyperwaste throughout the UK. Richard Cooper telling the managers any technical problems,

'Phone Vinson Chard.' The annoying thing being I was being paid a pittance this was galling I have difficulty selling myself with hindsight I should have demanded more at the time. Still the upside was I was now gaining more knowledge about the industry, and what I did not know, I would find out. During my time working at the plant, I was virtually in charge with Richard Cooper continually travelling the UK. Despite the poor pay, I enjoyed my time with the company, they were good days and the work was varied but certainly interesting to say the least, yet another high point in my career. The occasional demonstration helped liven things up somewhat and the arguments between Jamie and Cedric. Also other personnel began to use the facility as a base, such as Fred Germaine the Company Safety Officer.

When UPA eventually took over Hyperwaste outright, they thought it would be good idea for personnel morale to show some of the workforce the large incineration facility at Le May located on the outskirts of Paris. Hyperwaste personnel were randomly selected form all the sites throughout the UK, choosing approximately thirty eight of us at random. Cedric was chosen from the treatment plant to go on this excursion. Now for all his bluster, Cedric was not a particularly good mixer and declined the invitation to be one of the privileged 38. Instead Richard Cooper put my name forward. I was happy to go having only been once to Paris with Cindy quite few years earlier where we spent a romantic weekend. And so I was quite looking forward to it reliving old memories etc.

It meant driving to Manchester airport prior to the flight. Everyone congregated at the pre-arranged time of 12:00 for the flight to Paris. I drove, but some of the others from the other depots had taxis or minibuses arranged for them. We met at the departure lounge at about 11:45, although I arrived at about 11:30. As I had visited to some of the depots, I knew quite few people there. Amongst which was my old friend John Willis. Once we had all checked in, John suggested we have a drink at the bar, he twisted my arm and I agreed to have a pint of beer. After we had nearly consumed the first pint, John said we should have another one. It was whilst he made this suggestion, Tom Driscoll overheard us. At which point he interrupted with the comment.

'You do realize there are no toilets on the aircraft and will be at least a two hour flight?' I interrupted with the question but surely it only takes forty five minutes to fly to Paris?

81

Tom Driscoll, smiling at me, replied, 'Yes it does by jet, but these aircraft are turbo props and only take 19 passengers and will take about 2 hours to reach Paris. So I recommend you don't drink too much.'

Having an extremely low bladder capacity, I thought it prudent to accept his advice, although, I did think he was having a bit of a joke at suggesting the flight was by turboprop aircraft and was just winding us up, notwithstanding this I decided not to overtax my bladder just in case he was telling the truth. My old friend John Willis was having none of it, consuming a further two pints of beer before the flight.

We all boarded the two aircraft, both standing on the runway, and Tom Driscoll had not been joking, the aircraft were indeed two small turboprop aircraft, with limited carrying capacity, they looked like toys when alongside a Boeing 747 or 746 aircraft standing at the airport. As we entered our designated aircraft, most of us had to bend over slightly to avoid knocking our heads on the roof of the cabin.

Before the flight, our captain came in to explain the safety rules as specified by the CAA The frightening part of it was he was at least 6ft 6 inches tall and had to virtually bend over like an old man just to walk through the aircraft and he looked barely eighteen, although, in truth he must have been much older. He explained there should be very little passenger movement whilst the aircraft was in flight due to the instability caused by general movement within the aircraft.

The cabin was not pressurised and so the flight progressed at approximately 10,000 - 12,000 feet. When the cloud permitted, we could see the traffic travelling on the main vehicular arterial highways below us, it appeared to me the cars were actually travelling faster than we were. The flight seemed interminable cramped in that small aircraft. I remember my previous flight to Paris taking ¾ hour, at this rate it would take 2 - 2 1/2 hours. Any slight turbulence or increase in wind speed buffeted the tiny aircraft, which caused slight consternation, particularly to those with a morbid fear of flying.

After about 2 hours my bladder began experiencing the dire consequences of consuming one solitary pint of beer, but fortunately by this time I could just make out the outskirts of Paris below us realizing it would not be too long before we would be landing and the strain on my unfortunate bladder alleviated. Erroneously, I believed we would be landing at Charles De Gaulle airport, instead it appeared we would be landing at a small airport on the outskirts of Le May, near to where the major facility of UPA was situated. The aircraft had a somewhat bouncy landing, but after what seemed like an interminable amount of time and much to everyone's relief, the aircraft came to a standstill outside the small airport terminal. The other aircraft had already landed and the passengers already disembarked. I could see John Willis together with his other drinking partners making a frantic dash to the terminal pissoir, all appeared to be keeping their legs crossed, and trying to stop the urine which obviously expanded their bladders with tremendous pressure, from escaping and making an embarrassing exit down their trouser leg. My need was not so great having consumed less liquid and so was able to make a more dignified, sedate journey to the pissoir.

The night in the hotel was quite good with plenty to drink and eat. Everyone got to know each other, of course there were the usual characters and jokers who seemed to monopolise the conversation. Later we all split up into groups for excursions into the local town, unfortunately it being a Sunday there was not much going on, although some did get drunk and had to be awakened from their slumbers the next day for the trip to the headquarters of UPA at Le May.

The site was quite impressive it was a '*State of the Art*' large high temperature incinerator, fully capable of safely incinerating most waste such as PCB's pesticides, plastics, most organic compounds and all without emitting the dreaded, highly dangerous dioxins.

The only thing it could not incinerate were the red listed metals such as Mercury, Cadmium Arsenic which tend to go for landfill the facility even had its own landfill site nearby for the disposing of the filter cakes generated by the neutralization of the acid gasses formed during the incineration process.

We were shown all the facility and also met the chairman of UPA who was very personable and spoke impeccable English. However the same could not be said about his dress sensed he was the Chairman of UPA, yet his attire left a lot to be desired, he dressed like a sort of Jacques Tatti wearing a tight jacket and obviously too small for him, trousers just slightly too short 'flying at half mast,' as my mother used to say. His shoes were scuffed and unpolished, whilst his managers standing next to him such as Marcel Aymé and Tom Driscoll wore expensive, well-tailored, mohair suites, it was bizarre, this was the man in overall charge of the company? He gave us a talk about the history of his company UPA and how it became part of Regime De L'Aqua the giant parent company. He told us about the facility at Le May and the other facility in the South of France. It was fascinating stuff and we listened intently, his excellent English making him easy to understand.

That night we made the return flight to Manchester with Biggles Airlines. It being dark most of us had a slight snooze on the aircraft none of us had too much to drink remembering the outward flight. I eventually arrived home during the early hours of the morning, after a long, but exciting and interesting couple of days.

The same morning I returned to the treatment plant and the continual bickering between Jamie and Cedric, together with the banner waving demonstrators..... . Ah great joy.

CHAPTER 8

*J*amie Soames joined West Mercian Oil Refineries in the mid-seventies. As previously mentioned, he was another one of your typical hail-fellow, well-met sort of characters, the original cheeky chappy, easy to like and hard to dislike or find objectionable. He was the first person I met at the old WMO site, following its acquisition by Hyperwaste with his hearty greeting prior to my job interview, and during our discussion, Jamie helpfully advised me on how to impress and ingratiate my interrogators.

Jamie's nemesis and main adversary at the site tended to be Cedric. It was fun watching the two of them verbally sparring, trying to score points off each other, both vying for the approval, favouritism and approbation of Richard Cooper, gossiping and castigating the other at every given opportunity, whenever they (the other) made a mistake or an error of judgement. Richard Cooper, to his credit, tried not to give any favouritism to either one, just as a parent with rival siblings endeavours to keep the peace between them.

Besides Cedric, Jamie's other main obstacle in life tended to be his testosterone and hormone levels. For despite being in his mid-forties, Jamie appeared to have the hormones and testosterone of a seventeen year old teenager which he most definitely refused to give back. Jamie's nether regions, that is to say, his genitalia appeared to completely overrule anything his brain suggested or advise against, causing him all sorts of problems during his life.

Lorna, Jamie's wife, was absolutely gorgeous, extremely attractive, possessing a voluptuous figure accompanied by a wonderful, bubbly personality. As if that was not enough, she also managed to be extremely intelligent with a blossoming career and a well-paid job, a headmistress in one of the local junior schools. Yet, despite all of Lorna's feminine pulchritude and attributes, Jamie could not resist the alluring attraction of other members of the fairer sex, chatting up and flirting outrageously with any female wherever or whenever the opportunity presented itself. I must admit to being more than slightly envious of Jamie's unlimited ability to beguile and charm the opposite gender, which he appeared to do with consummate ease. Observing from the side-lines, as I often did, it appeared females absolutely adored him while, he in turn, schmoozed and charmed them. Yet, to me, Jamie appeared podgy and unattractive bearing an uncanny resemblance to Shrek the animated character. Then I am a mere male, what do I know which sort of man is attractive to women, unfathomable as the fairer sex is to our gender?

However, Jamie went far beyond chatting up, you could not describe him as *'All talk no action,'* in fact vice-versa when it came to my colleague and women. During those early months at the site, he was actually having an affair with Becky, a female friend he had known for years, although throughout most of his married life he had been unfaithful to Lorna on numerous other occasions, with a multitude of women.

When indulging in an extra marital affair, the participants generally try to keep the liaison quiet, desperately endeavouring to keep it as much of a secret as possible. However, in Jamie's case, everybody on site knew about it, mainly because he told all and sundry himself. Jamie was extremely proud of his libido and lady killing abilities, a fact he enjoyed broadcasting to all of his acquaintances.

For me to criticise my colleague is hypocritical. After all, had I not just two years earlier left my wife for the charms of another woman, as with Jamie, my testicles tended to override my brain. I am not castigating Jamie and his behaviour, just stating the facts. His affair with Becky was Jamie's downfall, for everything he did appeared to have the objective of meeting up with Becky for some extra marital nookie. Although extremely attractive, Becky could not hold a candle to his wife for charisma, charm and personality.

Jamie's affair caused a slight mishap during my time working for Hyperwaste at the treatment site. I had arranged to have some drums of solidified, waste resin collected from a haulage company based in the suburbs of Cardiff. After inspecting the drums and ascertaining the hazardous materials to be collected and approaching a local disposal site, I gave the manager a price which he found acceptable. A collection date was arranged with the client together with the Cardiff depot for the following week, after the hazardous waste 3 day pre-notification, section 17 had been complied with.

On the day of the collection, I had made a cock-up, assuming with the client being a transport company, they had their own forklift truck on site. Unfortunately, this was not the case, it being a tanker haulage company only, not requiring the use of such equipment as a fork truck. As agreed, the company vehicle appeared on site, but unfortunately, with no tail lift allowing the 'hand balling' of the drums onto the flatbed.

When the extremely agitated manager of the tanker company phoned, informing me he had no fork truck on his site, I quickly sprang into action locating a fork lift company, which fortuitously happened to be on the same industrial estate and in close proximity to the customer's premises. Following a bit of bartering over the phone, a price of twenty five pounds was eventually agreed for the use of a fork truck for about an hour. The only problem being we had to supply our own fork lift driver. At that time, I did not have a fork truck licence, but following a quick discussion with Richard Cooper, it was agreed, I could take Jamie with me as he possessed the necessary legal paperwork required for operating the vehicle.

Mistakenly, I thought Jamie would be pleased at being given the chance to get off site for a few hours and away from his nemesis, who invariably lorded it over him whenever they were on site together.

Upon informing Jamie of my plans for that particular afternoon, all I had was a mass of questioning such as how long it would take and would we be back before five o'clock. When I asked why he appeared to be in such a hurry to get back to the plant, especially with the possibility of some overtime in the offing. He quickly explained about a sexual assignation he had planned with Becky for that same evening. Lorna would be out for a number of hours, presenting Jamie with the opportunity of spending a few hours in the welcoming arms of his mistress, and sufficient time for indulging in adulterous, passionate, illicit fornication.

I eventually managed to placate him, explaining we would be back before five that evening, going through the planned itinerary in minute detail. Arranging to collect the fork truck at 2 p.m., drive it on the industrial estate around to the haulage company, which would take about 20 minutes, half an hour to load the vehicle, 20 minutes back, with an hour drive to the treatment plant. Well before five, allowing Jamie plenty of time to carry out his arranged tryst with his platinum blonde mistress. That was the plan. Unfortunately, as they say, 'the best laid plans.'

We arrived at the fork truck hire company at 1:45 p.m. only to find the person I had made the agreement with, the manager, not on site. No one else had the authority to give us the fork truck and knew nothing of our arrangement. Jamie became restless while I happily chatted to the attractive receptionist. I did it mainly to wind him up. He was so stressed about being late for his sexual liaison, his anxiety negating any interest he would normally have possessed in flirting with the pleasant and extremely cute, young lady on the reception desk.

Almost an hour passed before the manager eventually returned to the depot. After receiving the agreed cash amount, he gave us the keys for one of his diesel fork trucks. I told him we would bring it back as soon as possible. However, before we headed towards the waiting client, he did advise us, without giving a definitive explanation, not to drive the diesel fork truck too fast.

Jamie quickly boarded the fork truck and followed me around to the haulage company, where to our relief, the Hyperwaste vehicle and driver were waiting, after making a return journey from the Depot in Cardiff. The loading of the drums did not take long, Jamie manoeuvred the forks of the vehicle like a man possessed. At the treatment facility, his normal working speeds either comprised of slow or stop. It is surprising how enough of the right motivation can play a part in getting things done quickly.

After a short period of time, Jamie loaded all the drums of solidified resin onto the flatbed. Following a brief discussion with the client while getting the necessary legislative paperwork signed, we both headed back to the fork lift company. I drove ahead and Jamie followed behind in the ancient, dilapidated fork truck.

Arriving at the hire depot, I went to the reception area and awaited Jamie's arrival. With the manager being out, yet again, the opportunity presented itself to chat with the nice-looking receptionist, who, to say the least was extremely pleasant on the eye. Of course her feminine beauty, and the fact she was quite chatty and participated voluntarily in the conversation, made the time pass that much quicker. Before I realised it, over half an hour had passed by and still no sign of the over-sexed Jamie. It was now approaching 4:45, we should have been back at the treatment plant by now in accordance with Jamie's wishes and time line concerning his planned sexual activity with Becky. He had vociferously indicated he was keen to return to the plant as quickly as possible, and the fact he appeared to be taking so long in returning the fork truck indicated something must have occurred on his return journey to the depot. Making my apologies to the attractive receptionist, I got into the car and returned to the haulage company, taking the route we previously used. After travelling approximately half a mile, upon turning the corner I observed Jamie looking at the last flickering of dying flames, which, prior to my arrival had obviously totally engulfed the fork truck during their peak of colourful vibrancy. His expression was a mixture of crestfallen and panic. The vehicle now completely blackened and charred after what had obviously taken place moments earlier. It now stood on the side of the road completely useless, a mass of, burnt, buckled, soot covered, metal with protruding bare, electrical wiring.

'And where have you been?' He enquired angrily unable to avert his eyes from the catastrophe still faintly burning in front of him.

91

Before I had a chance to reply, Jamie then added sarcastically, 'Chatting up that receptionist I bet?'

I replied defiantly, more as a form of defence more than anything. 'Don't have a go at me. I bet you were speeding just so you could have your leg over with Becky?'

His lack of response meant I had hit the mark, he had indeed been pushing the truck to its limits to get back as soon as possible for his planned sexual liaison with Becky.

We each started to exhibit the hint of a smile.

'How the fuck, are we going to tell the guy at the hire company, he only loaned it to us as a favour?' I asked rhetorically and wondering what we were indeed going to do next and Richard Cooper would not take kindly to having to pay for the replacement of a fork truck.

We finally decided to return to the hire depot after first ensuring the flames had died away and completed their job of decimating the now defunct truck.

By the time, we returned to the hire company, the manager had returned from his excursion. Much to my relief, he took the whole incident in his stride, informing us, the insurance would take care of the damage, informing us the truck had been on its last legs anyway.

After giving him profuse apologies and explaining where he could locate his useless truck, we quickly vacated the site before he decided to change his mind and sue us. The remainder of the journey, for me anyway, was absolute purgatory having to endure the mutterings of Jamie, who complained vociferously about his missed opportunity to be with his beloved Becky. Informing me by the time we got back home, there would now be very little time to jump on his mistress' bones. Somehow, he managed to apportion the blame onto me for chatting to the receptionist telling me I should have looked for him much earlier. Although what I could have done is beyond me. It was evident his speeding had caused the whole incident, all because of his overactive libido and sex drive. After I put my case to him concerning his driving the fork truck far too fast to satisfy his sexual cravings, Jamie sulked and remained fairly silent for the remainder of the journey back to the treatment plant.

I considered the whole situation quite humorous, with Jamie blaming the whole incident on my somewhat limited charms used in chatting up a young female receptionist, when he was usually the one indulging in schmoosing and beguiling the females. I believe it took almost a week before we managed to converse as normal.

As with all affairs, Lorna discovered about Jamie's relationship with Becky, unsurprising really, the way he broadcast it to everyone. Their marriage ended in divorce and Jamie ultimately living with Becky, but not the entirely '*happy ever after*' scenario with Jamie bemoaning the fact wishing he was back with his wife after the Decree Absolute came through.

CHAPTER 9

*P*rior to working for my new employer, I had never heard of Cleckheaton, where one of the company depots managed to be situated. Not having the foggiest idea of its geographic location in the UK, finally discovering it to be on the outskirts of Leeds after being instructed to supervise the removal and disposal of hazardous chemicals for one of the large chemical companies located in Selby a few miles from the depot. My main point of contact at the Hyperwaste facility site turned out to be the Manager, Calvin Maynard, who had been made redundant from the same company which had also previously employed Tom Driscoll, our new Chief Executive. Being friends and ex-working colleagues, upon discovering Calvin's employment predicament, Tom offered him the position of Manager at the facility after the incumbent manager's termination of employment in the wake of the Chief Executive's management purge.

Calvin had only been working for the company a few months when we first met, hitting it off straight away, during a courtesy visit he made to the treatment plant. I found him personable, helpful, conscientious and always keen to do a thorough, professional job. The fact all the projects I performed on Calvin's behalf managed to be completed without any hiccups or mishaps, helped gain me esteem and a certain professional respect from the new manager, who had worked in the industry for a number of years and extremely knowledgeable when it came to the transportation of hazardous waste chemicals.

The Temporary Traffic Controller taking charge of operations during Calvin's absence over a few days, and which occurred during the time of this particular project, turned out to be a person named Fred Appleyard. Despite being in his fifties Fred tended to be a bit of a practical joker, always up to mischief and various pranks. Calvin instructed Fred to sort out accommodation for me during my time working at Selby. Being the comic he thought it would be great fun to put me in accommodation near '*the Clock,*' a fairly rough region of Leeds renowned for being endowed with one of the city's many Red Light districts, and consequently, full of undesirable, unsavoury characters, possessing quite a notorious, dangerous reputation. However, during my first and only night lodging in that particular, disreputable area of the city, I experienced no trouble whatsoever. When it came to Calvin's attention where Fred had actually booked accommodation for me, he tore him off a strip, informing him in no uncertain terms he should not have found me a hotel in such insalubrious a location. For my part, I tried informing Calvin it was no big deal and not to be so hard on his subordinate. Despite my protestations, Calvin created quite a stink about the affair and for the remainder of the project found lodgings more wholesome, decent and respectable, in a fairly large hotel, extremely comfortable, if somewhat expensive, but more importantly, in Calvin's mind, a far safer and more respectable area of the metropolis.

Calvin tended to panic when things went wrong and if there was anything technical or of a chemical nature, he invariably called upon my services, forever asking my advice such as which tankers should be used to carry certain chemicals. I had a terrible time job convincing him it was unacceptable to put 40% concentrated sulphuric acid into mild steel tanks but should be transported in stainless steel or lined tanks yet, paradoxically, acceptable to put the higher concentration of 98% acid into mild steel tanks. When he discovered I was correct he began transporting loads of highly concentrated sulphuric acid in mild steel tankers, his admiration for me knew no bounds, this fact enabled him to make better utilisation of his tanker fleet, allowing him more flexibility when planning transportation schedules.

He also seemed to have more problems than most of the other managers and not always to do with chemicals or of a technical nature. Such an instance occurred one summer. Being the silly season of the summer months, when many drivers booked their annual vacations. To make up this short fall in his staff, Calvin tended to hire agency drivers. One year, he hired an agency driver in his early fifties, mostly utilised in taking the fairly innocuous materials for disposal, i.e. transported as non-hazardous materials. One such consignment consisted of thousands of 300 ml glass bottles containing a soft orange drink. The drinks, from a well-known soft drinks company, had somehow become contaminated with slivers of broken glass during processing. The glass contamination meant the whole production batch became designated for landfill after first being crushing on the disposal site. During a period of time in the late eighties and early nineties, liquids could be disposed of at some of the landfill sites, then an acceptable practice, now no longer permitted under revised waste legislation.

Unfortunately, while transferring the contaminated soft drinks to the designated landfill site in Cumbria, the agency driver suffered a massive heart attack, which sadly, proved fatal. The myocardial infarction (heart attack) occurred while he was driving the articulated vehicle, causing it to overturn. Some innocent motorists were also injured when the lorry, completely out of control, collided with their vehicles. Of course the police became involved and the post mortem ascertained the driver had indeed died whilst at the wheel due to the massive heart attack he had sustained. The traffic accident was nobody's fault, such as a result of dangerous or drunken driving, just one of those unfortunate occurrences.

From here on in this is where it became difficult for Calvin. The agency driver had parked his car in the company car park before beginning his last, fateful shift. All drivers left their car keys in the office, in case their vehicle required moving for some reason which is what he did.

A few days following the agency driver's demise, a woman turned up at the site requesting the keys for his vehicle, claimed to be his wife. As proof, she showed Calvin her spouse's driving licence. Of course with the driver being an agency driver, Calvin had no idea about his personal life or relatives. Calvin handed the car keys over to the woman, who immediately drove the vehicle away

The next day, a different woman appeared at the premises requesting the keys for the same car, this woman also claimed to be the wife of the deceased agency driver. Calvin did not know what to do as he had already given the keys to the other woman the previous day and she had taken the car away.

He made a frantic phone call to Steve Charles, the personnel director asking his advice on the unusual predicament. The Personnel Director told Calvin that the woman should provide him with proof of her relationship with the dead driver, which she did, also showing Calvin their marriage licence. The woman went ballistic after being informed the car had been handed over to the other woman. It appeared the first woman was in fact the driver's girlfriend, with whom he now shared a love nest after leaving his wife, the second woman, some months earlier. The woman now glared at Calvin through malevolent eyes. All Calvin could do was to apologise profusely and suggest she take matters up with the mistress and sort it out between themselves. The woman eventually left, much to Calvin's relief, with steam metaphorically venting from every orifice.

Unfortunately for Calvin, the story did not end there, a few days later, a third woman appeared at the depot also asking for the car, yet another girlfriend, of whom, apparently, the other two women had no inkling. Calvin threw his hands up in despair and told her if she wanted the car to sort it out with the other two female acquaintances of the deceased driver. I think during the following days, he half expected a fourth woman to manifest herself, also asking for the same popular vehicle.

I have heard of sailors having a girl in every port, but this driver appeared to have a girl in every town. No wonder he suffered a heart attack, between the stress of being involved with three women and endeavouring to keep them carnally satiated, his body must have given up in despair.

Most people have a hobby or interest, or something which really interests them and pushes their buttons, in the case of Calvin this turned out to be a street called Lumb Lane located in Bradford. The street featured in a drama series called Band of Gold about prostitutes in that particular area of the city. While working on another project and staying in Cleckheaton, Calvin offered to have a meal with me one night, arranging to collect me from the hotel so that I could have a few drinks. As agreed he picked me up and took me to an Indian restaurant situated in Bradford, which, by coincidence, was located at the end of the aforementioned street. We both ate our highly spiced meals which in my case, as I recall ended up being chicken Pathia, pillau rice with peshwari naan and chutney tray with popadoms. After consuming the rather large meal, Calvin casually suggested he show me the sites in Lumb Lane, although he specified, we would not be availing ourselves of the services on offer, just the shilling tour. We drove down the street, with Calvin pointing out the young girls involved in the business, often described, together with doctors, as the oldest profession in the world.

Calvin possessed the ability and knowledge to point out all the girls. He knew their names and any TV programmes or documentaries in which they had appeared regarding the infamous street. His knowledge pertaining to the thoroughfare knew no bounds, seemingly virtually limitless. He could have appeared on mastermind. Images of the popular TV programme often generated in my psyche, with Magnus Magnusson saying, 'Your specialised subject is Lumb Lane and the prostitutes of Bradford.'

To any observer, his car must have appeared to contain a couple of guy's kerb crawling as it slowly cruised along the street, while Calvin continually pointed out the individual girls. He appeared to be completely unfazed by the police cars strategically located along the notorious street. It came as surprise to me the police never pulled Calvin in for kerb crawling. Finally, Calvin decided it was time to leave the disreputable street and call it a night, but only after I had been given the life story of virtually every prostitute touting for business along the road. I thought it amusing after he had given Fred such a rough time about putting me in a hotel slap bang in the middle of a similar area, and here he was deliberately taking me to yet another one.

The next morning I called into the depot, and began chatting to Angela, the middle-aged receptionist. When I told her I had a meal with Calvin that previous evening, she casually asked me if he had shown me the sites of Lumb Lane. I looked at her somewhat dumbfounded and, to be quite honest, slightly embarrassed, not knowing how to reply.

'Don't worry,' she said, a broad smile appearing on her face upon observing my discomfort.

'That's Calvin's entertainment for the customers and Hyperwaste personnel, he just loves taking people down the Lane. We all know he does it, even Helen his wife. We're only surprised by the fact he hasn't been arrested for kerb crawling.'

'Me too,' I replied, relieved Angela did not consider me to be a pervert. Although, Angela being middle aged, fairly attractive and, I suspect, quite worldly wise, not at all shocked by Calvin's hobby. I think however she would have been shocked had I availed myself of the services on offer down the Lane. Angela then carried on quite nonchalantly with her work.

I hate hypocrisy, and one event of which Calvin informed me created a new impression in my mind concerning two company directors. I had been instructed to attend a technical, sales meeting in a prestigious Birmingham hotel. The day prior to driving to the meeting, I received a phone call from Calvin, asking if I could bring up a box containing a couple of dozen 500 millilitre glass sample jars for him to use on a large project which the Depot intended tendering for. Upon reaching the car park of the hotel, I observed Calvin driving into the parking lot and waited for him, to transfer the sample jars into the boot of his car. While we were in the process of doing this, Steve

Charles, The Personnel Director walked past us and acknowledged me with a cheery 'Good Morning Vinson.' Although greeting me, Steve completely ignored my colleague.

With Steve out of earshot, Calvin remarked, 'Ignorant, hypocritical bastard, he's too ashamed to acknowledge me since the incident with Tina and Ian Smith.'

I looked at him bemused. 'What's all that about?' I enquired, thoroughly intrigued by his remark.

'You really don't know?'

There was no reticence as far as Calvin was concerned about the subject and he immediately went into a monologue concerning the mysterious topic.

'Well, you remember Ian Smith, the Waste manager from Teesside?'

I nodded to affirm I knew Ian, although I realised it was a rhetorical question on his part.

'He had no secretary to do his accounts and paperwork, so every few weeks, he would come down to Cleckheaton and Tina, my secretary, would do all the accounts and any typing for the Teesside depot. Well after a while, he and Tina began having an affair, of which I had no knowledge whatsoever. That is until I was summoned to head office in Manchester and a meeting with Tom Driscoll and Steve Charles. They both gave me a right dressing down and accused me of condoning the relationship. Telling me how they valued family values and would not tolerate such immoral behaviour. They virtually blamed me and told me I should have put a stop to it. I told them I had no knowledge, to which they accused me of lying and knowing what was going on in the depot. They told me I had to sack Tina. I refused at first, but they said if I didn't they would and I might go as well. It seemed

101

when I phoned her, she was actually in bed with Ian at the time.'

I looked at him and waited for him to continue.

'Is that it?' I enquired, convinced he had more information to impart.

He then went on. 'Well no, I'm coming to it, a few weeks later Tom Driscoll actually caught Steve Charles and his secretary Lynne, *flagrante delicto* in his office, on the desk apparently, with her legs wrapped tightly around his back. The upshot being Lynne was also sacked. It seems in this company, the secretaries are always the scapegoats and first for the chop. Of course the women will not take it to a tribunal because they do not want to rock the boat because of their husbands. So there you have it, Steve gave me a right dressing down for something I had no knowledge of, giving me a lecture on promiscuity extolling family values and all that, while all the time he was having it off with Lynne, his secretary. Since that day, he has not said a word to me.... As I said, fucking hypocrite.'

With that final statement Calvin ended his monologue, still cursing Steve Charles under his breath, as we walked into the hotel foyer. From that day on, I had a completely different view of our illustrious leaders, agreeing with Calvin concerning their hypocrisy.

There were a number of customers belonging to the Cleckheaton depot whose waste I would occasionally sort and label for shipment. In the early nineties, the waste had to be put into reasonable containers for shipment, mostly 45 gallon drums, either bung clip tops, steel or plastic. It was so easy in those early days to categorise the waste for shipment, with only 17 general labels in use categorising the waste as liquid or solid, then acid, alkali, toxic, flammable or oil. However as the decade progressed the law concerning the shipment and disposal of waste became more stringent with the identification of the waste becoming more specific, resulting in excess of 3,000 possible types of labels and identification using UN numbers. I was fortunate to be in at the outset, growing up with the more stringent legislation and so became in even more demand throughout the depots.

I began ordering all the new white papers and legislative documents when the Parliamentary laws concerning the waste industry came into being, advising the depots as to which UN numbers were required for identification of the waste. Most of the people involved with Hyperwaste, with it being a transport company, were hauliers by nature who just happened to be involved with transportation of hazardous waste. But the legislation was becoming more demanding and more specialised. Even the sales guys were not chemists and so my job became more challenging as I tended to be consulted more and more about the movement of various types of waste. Following some people leaving the company such as Malcolm Roundtree and Richard Mainwaring, I gradually became the person with the most chemical knowledge within Hyperwaste throughout the UK, necessitating travelling extensively around the country, particularly as the treatment site was not being utilised for its purpose of treating waste. Meanwhile the legal arguments between Local Council, the Welsh Development Agency and Hyperwaste dragged on, much to the lawyer's glee. My job while at the treatment facility, tended to be a mixture of being 'hands on,' donning overalls and dealing with waste at the coal front so to speak and then the next day wading through documents and the proposed legislation and implemented new acts to understand and interpret them ensuring Hyperwaste did not break the any laws carrying out chemical analysis, answering technical queries. Stella did not seem to mind me being away during the week, as long as I was home on the weekends.

Because of my growing knowledge, Calvin utilised me as much as possible. One regular job involved dealing with the waste at a large chemical company near Leeds, having to spend a sometime on the customer's premises. The person I dealt with was as corrupt as they come, making no bones about other companies not taking him out for lunch and wining and dining him at expensive restaurants which Calvin told me I should do to butter him up as much as possible, I suspect the rep from Cleckheaton would also bribe him with hard cash. The contract with the chemical company was worth hundreds of thousands each year and so a few quid here and there was well worth it in the eyes of Calvin Maynard and the local sales representative, and probably with the approval of the directors. Yes, undoubtedly, a lot of that certainly goes on within the waste industry, and many other industries besides.

CHAPTER 10

*T*he years moved along, 1989 changing into 1990 which itself became 1991. The antipathy and stalemate between Hyperwaste, the residents and the local council continued unabated, with demonstrations against the plant and its operation, helping liven up the days at the facility, when masses of belligerent, angry, placard waving groups of protestors suddenly appearing, as if by magic, outside the gates, their numbers swollen by corrupt councillors hoping to gain financially by the closure of the plant and local members of parliament, eager to gain some political mileage from the whole situation, possessing no altruistic or philanthropic intent on their part.

At the time, I had plenty of work to do, despite the fact that we were not allowed to treat waste already transferred to the facility or receive any further waste on site. I still had to complete setting up and improving the laboratory, answer the telephones, write analytical procedures for the new quality system, answer technical queries from the various depots located throughout the UK, analyse the waste samples which continually arrived from the technical sales representatives and especially Richard Mainwaring for the first few months. Interspersed with my time on site, I continually travelled to the various sites throughout the UK and work on waste projects, packaging waste for shipment or supervise chemical cleaning operations. I was not bored in the slightest and having a thoroughly enjoyable time and at that time still in a new relationship with Stella and still in the honeymoon period with the additional bonus of enjoying going to work every day, apart from cantankerous Cedric that is, but then you can't have everything.

Interspersed with all this, we had visits from new employees who had recently joined the company, mostly Tom Driscoll's friends and acolytes from his previous company. Then there were the exorbitantly paid solicitors and barristers acting on Hyperwaste's behalf who would occasionally visit the site, travelling from their offices in London, putting lots of questions in order to prepare their case for the company against the local council. Their fees included the journey time from and back to London, by first class rail of course.

The plant also received visits from the regulatory authorities such as the NRA, which years later became incorporated into the Environment Agency. The plant had an interceptor on site for preventing any oil from discharging into the sewage system and the NRA had the responsibility of monitoring the plant. One morning we received a visit from the area manager for the NRA, who turned out to be an old school friend, who had also previously been responsible for monitoring the Repeat Control Corporation manufacturing facility at Brynmawr when he worked for Welsh Water, the waste treatment section then became part of the NRA. We had a good rapport and working relationship, particularly after Repeat Controls with a new treatment plant being successfully installed. It was a pleasant and welcome surprise to see him on site. We had a good old chat reminiscing about the old school days and friends we used to know. It is always handy to have an old school friend working for the regulatory authorities, not that we did anything wrong but if advice were required then it is much easier when dealing with an old friend using the old boy network.

Although the case for issuing a site licence still had not been agreed, the company still had planning permission for installation of new process equipment which had been granted in 1989 due to an oversight on the part of the council's planning department. So Hyperwaste continued with the installations for which the planning permission had been granted. Slowly the new additions to the plant began taking shape, particularly the new clarifier required for settling, inert, neutral sludge prior to filtration through the plate and frame filter press. The clarifier, although not huge by the standards of most sewage treatment plants throughout the country, created quite an impressive sight with the capability of holding half a million gallons or two thousand cubic metres of liquid. Upon completion in June 1990, the clarifier had to be hydraulically tested to ensure it could withstand the volume and weight of liquid contained in it. The only way to do this practically meant filling the newly completed, huge cylindrical process tank with water from the mains. It actually took a couple of days to fill the clarifier to the required intended normal operating level. Latham Engineering performed a wonderful, competent engineering job in constructing the clarifier and so it became evident the numerous riveted plates had no leaks whatsoever and the whole edifice contained the huge amount of water with no difficulty at all.

Within a few days of the clarifier being filled with fresh water, drivers from the Cardiff depot kept turning up on site for minor problems with their vehicle for the fitters to rectify. The weather at the time tended to be very hot and humid and the drivers began bringing their swimming costumes to take a dip in the fresh cold water. Jamie also began bringing his swimming costume to work, using the huge clarifier as a swimming pool at the end of the day. It became evident the drivers began turning up at the end of the day with the most minor complaints relating to their vehicles, just for a dip in the cool clarifier water. This extra influx of drivers tended to shorten the working day with extra people to talk to besides Cedric and Jamie. However, I had to advise Richard to stop the aquatic activities after a while, fearing a build-up of bacteria in the water, which did not please the drivers.

Indeed this time in my working life tended to be unusual and quite eclectic, with differing events and circumstances, nevertheless, very enjoyable. I got to know quite a few of the people working for Hyperwaste, either through their visits to the plant, or through my extensive travelling of the country, visiting the numerous depots. I was once asked by somebody prior to Hyperwaste, 'Describe a typical working day.' Typical was most certainly a word you could not use to describe my working day at Hyperwaste, for with each day I never knew what could occur or transpire, but it certainly stopped me getting bored.

Many events occurred at this time so it is difficult to recall with complete accuracy which episode materialized and when. Certainly a lot of Hyperwaste directors and managers came and went during that first year, indeed some so fast I did not even get to know their names. The major casualties as far as I was concerned being Richard Mainwaring, who thought he was a law unto himself, continually arguing with Tom Driscoll in front of other managers and directors at meetings. There was a distinct antipathy between them both and so after Richard's mentors Dave Parry and Samuel Abbott had both been removed by the main French Company UPA, he then shortly followed, after he had made certain secret deals with other companies and lining his pockets at Hyperwaste's expense before his employment with the company was eventually terminated. The last I saw of Richard was just after he had been dismissed. He had loaned me some expensive chemical textbooks concerned with water treatment and unable to collect them after his dismissal and not permitted to enter any Hyperwaste sites. We arranged to meet in Newport before I went to look at a waste disposal job in Cardiff. I did not inform anyone in Hyperwaste in case the meeting and my reasons becoming misconstrued with me still being in contact with the former Manager. I handed him the expensive text books. He bought me breakfast and spent the whole meal castigating Tom Driscoll and others including Dave Pearce. There was obviously no love lost between them all. We shook hands I thanked him for giving me my job and then said goodbye. That was the last time I ever saw Richard Mainwaring, never having seen him since.

The next to go was Dave Moreland. I liked Dave, he was your Dell Boy, flash, spiv type, but likeable. Driving around in his company car, a Porsche 911 he instilled just that image. Dave loved his Porsche and when Tom Driscoll dismissed him in the latter part of 1990 he insisted the Porsche went with him as part of his settlement. I was sad to see him go as we got on well together. The person most upset about Dave's Departure was Richard Cooper, not only did they have a good working relationship, but they were good friends as well.

As predicted, by some perspicacious personnel, within a few weeks of Dave Moreland's departure, the position of Area Director became redundant and a new supremo Director of UK Sales established with Dave Pearce, the consultant elevated to the new position.

Dave Pearce, almost immediately began establishing himself, his time as waste consultant had been well utilized, he had delved into the operation of the company and knew which personnel he wanted to go and those who would stay. Thankfully I had not alienated him when he first joined the company unlike many others. The company had two separate divisions, Waste Management and Industrial Cleaning. Dave Pearce, was not fully cognizant of the Industrial section but knew the actual waste very well and so concentrated on that division. The headquarters for the industrial Division had been based at Port Talbot, within close proximity to The Port Talbot Steelworks where they had a large contract, unfortunately and disastrously, in the summer of 1990, they lost the main contract for the steelworks which amounted to almost 80% of the business for Port Talbot. The offices at Port Talbot were gradually depleted, with some of the Industrial Managers basing themselves at the treatment facility, amongst them was a guy called Greg Polanski. Others were also made redundant. Richard Cooper as well as looking after the treatment plant was given the job of trying to claw back some of the business lost by Port Talbot and put in charge of the Industrial Division, he had no chance from the outset, with the major contract being lost at Port Talbot Steelworks. His position of Area Manager for waste was taken over by Dave Pearce who concentrated on the waste disposal.

It was not obvious to me at that time, but Richard Cooper did not get on too well with Dave Pearce and he did not have the same working relationship and rapport he had generated with Dave Moreland. The circumstances of which will be explained in later chapters.

There is a sad story concerning one of the depots located in Hertfordshire, previously owned by a family the father, his wife and son and it shows the heartlessness of the business world. The family made a reasonable living out of collecting septic tank waste from the rural houses and farms in the area not on mains sewage and which proliferated the area then taking the waste to the local sewage works. The family up until that time only answerable to the banks. Somehow, the father and son had become friendly with Richard Mainwaring who persuaded the family to sell out to Hyperwaste during the company's expansion and acquisition period. They eventually agreed and became managers of the depot. Hyperwaste had plans for the depot to deal with Hazardous waste and toxic waste. Unfortunately the family were not knowledgeable about the hazardous waste industry and not generating the business which Richard Mainwaring had forecast. I gave them assistance when dealing with hazardous material and how it should be shipped and packaged etc. But they had to generate the work and contacts in the area. Unfortunately after about six months, during the financial problems within Hyperwaste, the depot had not produced the profits forecast and all three of the family were made redundant and paid off. I accidently phoned the depot just after they had been given their notices and talked to the wife who was very bitter, vehemently criticising Richard Mainwaring and what he had done to them and how he had affected their lives.

Shortly afterwards, Len Protheroe was brought in as manager to try and bring in the extra business. Len was another person who had previously worked with both Tom Driscoll and Dave Pearce and great friends with both of them. He told them he was having problems with Richard Cooper and of course they took Len's side, Richard Cooper was then moved sideways to the industrial section and given the impossible task of reviving the dying business, whilst still having responsibility for the treatment plant. In all fairness Richard Cooper put in the hours to desperately try to revive the doomed division.

111

Throughout the latter part of 1990 and the beginning of 1991, Dave Pearce began to turn up more and more at the treatment facility. He began involving me in the new impending hazardous waste legislation and the new laws about to be implemented concerning the identification of waste and chemicals for shipment.

Dave Pearce was forever looking at ways to diversify and make money for the company but also looking towards the future concerning his personal esteem within the corporation, probably with the future intention of becoming Managing Director when Tom Driscoll either left or received promotion within UPA. One of his projects involved putting in a tender for recycling waste oils contained in lagoons at the enormous ICI site at Wilton near Middlesbrough. There were seven lagoons in total each holding hundreds of thousands of tonnes of miscellaneous oils, some contained heavy fuel oils which sank to the bottom, others contained lighter oils on the top, with light solids amongst the oils and of course dirty, rancid water. There were rumours concerning the lagoons before they had been properly sealed off and a security system installed, people often used the area by the lagoons as a short cut from Redcar after drinking in the numerous local pubs. Being late at night and often pitch black it is believed a number of missing people wandered into the lagoons and quickly drowned in the oils. My fear was I would unearth a body during the sampling operation. Not only humans but all sorts of animals such as squirrels, foxes, rabbits and even dogs, had often been seen to drown in the lagoons.

To enable Hyperwaste to put in an accurate tender for the recycling and burning of the oils, it became necessary for samples to be taken of each of the lagoons at various locations to obtain accurate representation of the mix of oils and then ascertain which type of separation process would be the most efficient for recovering the oils to be burnt in the boilers used at Wilton, saving ICI hundreds thousands of pounds in fuel costs.

I was instructed to spend some time at the Wilton site taking samples from the lagoons. For me to sample from various locations in each of the seven huge lagoons, I bought a hollow sampling stick with a number of connecting pieces. The first piece had a ball valve in it, when the stick dropped vertically into the liquid, allowed the valve to open, as the stick dropped into the liquid. The oil slowly seeped into the hollow stick, giving virtually a representative sample throughout the depth of the liquid in the lagoons. When the stick was pulled out of the liquid, the ball dropped to the bottom of the stick stopping the collected liquid from seeping out of the tube. The sampling tube proved to be very simple to operate, yet ingeniously efficient. Sections of the tube screwed into each other extending the length as required, similar to the way the old chimney sweep extended the length of his chimney brush, increasing the length of the sampling stick required dependent upon the depth of the liquid in the particular lagoon. To drop the stick into the lagoons, it was necessary to hire a huge crane which lifted the stick vertically into the air, then dropped it slowly into the lagoon at locations designated by myself. When the sampling stick was lifted out it contained the oil sludge. Some of the lagoons required a total sampling length of 5 metres, almost 15 feet in old money. The tricky part was to empty the contents from the hollow sampling tube into gallon jacks, the crane driver slowly dropped the stick onto the ground until it became almost horizontal and I would then gingerly empty the contents from the open end into the container, careful not to spill any. This operation was repeated time and time again as I tried to get representative samples from various locations of each lagoon. It was February 1991 and the weather consequently thoroughly miserable, mostly, cold, wet and windy. The lagoons were exposed to the elements. Because of the nature of the work, I found it was necessary to wear an industrial wet suit, gauntlets wellingtons, goggles and safety helmet. Each evening I went back to the Billingham Arms thoroughly cold and miserable where I was joined most evenings by my old friend John Willis who would have a quite few drinks with me before his wife collected him. This operation went on for a full week. On the last day I needed to get a few samples from the last lagoon and almost finished by 3:30 that afternoon. Dave Pearce drove to the area with Tom Driscoll, showing him the scope of the work and his intentions to set up an oil recovery plant on the site. I must have looked a pitiful sight, slowly trudging along the mud covered, saturated road, wrapped up in my yellow, industrial wet suit desperately, trying to protect myself from the torrential, driving rain, my Wet suit blackened and liberally covered with all sorts of oils from the lagoons. Dave Pearce stopped his car lowered his window which I approached. He enquired how it was progressing. By lowering his car window, Dave began experiencing the full force of the driving rain on his face. I had my wet suit hood up with the rain blowing against my back. As he tried talking to me I could see both his eyes blinking uncomfortably and frantically as the rain blew into them at high velocity. I informed him the job was nearly complete and that I had two more samples to take which should be done within the hour. The cheeky sod then said to me, 'I suppose you'll be heading off to South Wales when that's done?'

I became quite belligerent. 'No,' I replied, 'I am thoroughly cold, wet and miserable, the last thing I want is a six hour drive on top. I plan to return to the Billingham Arms for a nice meal with a few beers before returning home in the morning.'

Dave could see I had a point and made no further comment, just nodding his head in agreement. I had been on the site since 8:30 that morning and could not face the prospect of a six hour drive.

I was pleased the following week after collating all the lagoon samples I had taken. I had worked quite hard and taken numerous samples. Hyperwaste involved Alpha Laval, a centrifuge company for separating the oils and water, after it became evident there was far too much solid content for just one or two centrifuges which would require a battery of them which are not cheap and so the costs tended to be on the high side for ICI who approached another company which wanted to use heat and settlement tanks. So Hyperwaste did not get the contract which was just as well, because Dave Pearce had planned for me to run the operation. I did not fancy the prospect of moving up to the North East. I knew Stella certainly would not relocate had Hyperwaste won the contract.

From the middle of 1991, activity and visits by Hyperwaste Personnel, officials from the council and lawyers to the treatment Plant appeared to diminish somewhat and things became quiet. One day Greg Polanski called me into his office, as previously mentioned, with the closure of The Port Talbot Offices, Greg relocated to the plant. He had decided to have a clean-up and began going through his old files on industrial cleaning.

'Have a look at that Vinson,' he said pointing to a large sheet which he had pinned to the board in his office, I detected a hint of sadness and regret in his voice.

I looked at it, observing it to be a Hyperwaste Industrial division management tree for the South Western Region, which apparently so Greg informed me included South Wales down to the south coast of England. The management tree evidently included quite a large amount of personnel, I estimate with driver's sales people and other personnel indicated on the sheet it must have amounted to over sixty people.

Greg spoke, 'You would never believe it but I had all those people working for me at one time'

'How many work for you now?' I enquired.

'No-one just me,' he replied with a hint of regret and bewilderment at the sudden demise of his previously extensive empire. Greg was responsible for sales in the industrial cleaning for south Wales and the west, and had no-one now reporting to him, not even a secretary.

'I don't think I will be with Hyperwaste much longer at this rate.'

'Naah!' I replied trying to boost his flagging morale and self-esteem, adding 'They probably have plans for you.'

A fortnight later those plans revealed themselves but not the way I expected but in the way Greg had forecast. It was a sunny, hot cloudless day at the plant and for once I was not required to be elsewhere and concentrated on analysing some samples which had been brought in by some reps from the waste division. Quite a few people suddenly turned up on site, including my old mate Fred Germaine who had been absent for quite a while due to his duties with Health and Safety and BS 5740 elsewhere in the United Kingdom.

'Hello Fred,' I said to him, 'long time no see, what brings you to plant?'

'I have a meeting with Dave Pearce, along with a few others.' The others I learnt included Greg and quite a few of the sales representatives, including, Dave Moreland's Cousin and another relative of his, John Davies who worked out of Llanelli.

Just before noon, Dave Pearce arrived on site and one by one they went in to have a chat with him, and one by one they came out with, despondent, gloomy expressions on their faces. Evidently Dave was performing his required task, namely, that of hatchet man, sacking them all one by one. Just like other companies I had worked for, it was another '*night of the long knives*'.

The first to be informed was Geoff Jones, a waste representative who worked around the Gloucester area. He looked as if he could burst into tears when he emerged from his meeting with Dave.

Dave came out of the meeting room immediately behind Geoff and approached me.

'Vinson, do me a favour,' he said with no hint of remorse at what he had just done to Geoff's career within the company.

'Geoff's company car is low on fuel, could you fill it up with Diesel for him, and he doesn't know how to operate the pump.'

I instructed Geoff to drive his car to the diesel pump which we had on site.

He parked his company car to the pump, got out of his vehicle and did not say a word.

I did not know what to say to him guessing what had taken place during his meeting with Dave Pearce, and proceeded filling the car without speaking a word. If he wished to talk, I would let him

Speak first, which he never did, until I finished putting the diesel into the tank.

Then before he got into his car, Geoff shook my hand, thanked me, and wished me all the best, got into his company car and drove away as quickly as he could.

None of the others required diesel in their cars, but left as quickly as possible after being informed of their fate by Dave Pearce. All of them did, however come and say farewell to me before they left for the last time.

One particular depot manager on the south coast received a visit from Dave Pearce at the depot. He had four weeks grace in which he could have use of his company vehicle, a 4 x 4. When the time came for him to hand the vehicle back to the company, he refused and continued driving the vehicle for his personal use. After a while, it became necessary for Dave to go to his house accompanied by bailiffs in order to retrieve the vehicle. The manager Derek barricaded himself in his house and refused to emerge. The bailiff had to break into the 4 x 4 and then winch it onto a tow truck to take it back up north. I felt sad to see so many good people being sacked, wondering how long before I met the same fate, the way things appeared to be going, not long, I thought.

The engineering contractor performed wonders, transforming the plant which now had the capability of treating thousands of gallons of waste which Hyperwaste had anticipated, with everything nearly complete and ready for operation, the shame of it being, we were still prohibited from receiving and treating industrial waste on the site. Richard Cooper kept the clarifier full of water. Which the drivers used for a few weeks as a swimming pool until I advised against it for fear of the drivers catching some dreaded disease.

Ominously there appeared to be less and less activity around the plant, also the previously frequent visits from Dave Pearce appeared to be more and more scarce coupled with the fact Richard Cooper also appeared to be away from the plant quite a lot, although Dave kept saying he wanted me to become a sort of technical advisor for the company. I began perusing the Western Mail job section, once again fearing the worse, another change of job appeared to be looming on the horizon and I thought I had better be a bit pro-active. I remembered how Jim Gunn at Cox & Sons kept a low profile before the axe finally fell, and this seemed to be the exact same scenario.

Of course, Cedric kept coming up with his theories as to what was happening, all of which proved to be incorrect.

CHAPTER 11

*I*t was now approaching the end of 1991 and Hyperwaste had been at the facility since June 1989, not bad when you consider all the demonstrations, together with the adverse publicity and press coverage which the plant had received, throughout that time, with the imminent threat of the facility closure forever threatening on the horizon, yet we were all still there. The company had been through numerous hearings and court cases, finally appealing to the Welsh Office. After numerous discussions, the Welsh Office ruled in favour of Hyperwaste, stating the company had every right to remain and operate the site and treat the industrial waste oils, acids and alkalis, despite being in the middle of the prestigious Garden Festival site with its inauguration rapidly approaching and still designated for the summer of 1992. Personally, it is my opinion, the extreme right wing Tory Welsh minister John Redwood came down on the side of Hyperwaste, in all probability, to piss off and upset the socialist labour council which held political power in the region. Whatever the reasons, the Welsh Office passed the judgement stating, the company could remain and operate from the old West Mercian Oil site, the judgement also stipulated, Hyperwaste had every right to be there and should be granted a site licence without any more delay, for the disposal of toxic waste generated by industry. The ramifications of this edict meant, in order to persuade Hyperwaste to vacate the site, the council would have to pay dearly.

Dave Pearce, had acquired the reputation of being, *the hatchet man* because he had sacked so many of my

120

colleagues, including my old friends Fred Germaine and Greg Polanski during the day of the long knives, the day when quite a few managers and sales representatives suddenly turned up unexpectedly on site, each one had a one to one meeting with Dave. As each emerged one by one from their meetings, every one of them exhibited the same dour, melancholy expressions after being informed of their termination of employment. I cannot say it came as a surprise, the company was in the red once again. With barrister's fees, of which there were three, running at £400 per barrister per hour including travelling time from and back to London for visits to the plant, also the exorbitant salaries of the old guard including Dave Parry, Dave Moreland, Richard Mainwaring, and Samuel Abbott and their severance pay but there was more pruning to be done, a dirty job for which Tom Driscoll had specifically brought in his old friend Dave Pearce. I acquired an invaluable lesson from this time. Do your job but do not get too close to the top people. Before my time at Hyperwaste came to an end there were to be a number of regimes, each ridding personnel from the previous one and settling old scores. Being just an underling, I managed to stay employed. The company was now beginning to look far different from the one I initially joined and a number of people from Tom's previous employment began appearing in high management and executive positions, all Dave's former colleagues. I appeared to be main person in the company with chemical Engineering experience and knowledge so appeared to be quite safe for the time being. The others were transport managers and salesmen. The only person from the previous regime who managed to keep his job was Richard Cooper mainly because he was personable, hard-working, conscientious but the main reason being, he was

121

invaluable and the mainstay of the plant. The truth was, Dave Pearce needed him and unable to manage without him, at least for the time being. By now Richard was Manager for the whole of the UK waste section.

Things became extremely quiet and so I had decided to book three weeks holiday for Christmas. We were prohibited from treating any waste and there appeared to be a lull in my requirements around the country.

About lunchtime one afternoon in late November, I received a phone call from Richard Cooper instructing me to meet him and Dave Pearce at the Port Talbot Depot and to be there by 4 pm. My heart started to beat ten to the dozen. When Dave Pearce requested a meeting, it could only mean one thing, the probability of once again being re-acquainted with my P45. Ah well, I thought, I had at least stopped the run of being unemployed after a few months, it had now been almost two and a half years since I first joined Hyperwaste, *c'est la vie* as they say. I even tidied my desk before getting into the car and making my way to the Port Talbot depot. I arrived at the Port Talbot Depot which was being run down due to the loss of the contract for the Port Talbot Steelworks, the depot ran the industrial cleaning operations at the gargantuan steelworks at Port Talbot. When I told, the staff I had a meeting with Dave Pearce, all they could utter in shock being the single word 'Oh!' knowing full well Dave's previous recent history for sacking Hyperwaste personnel at the drop of a hat.

I waited nervously at the office trying to act calm talking to the people I knew. During our telephone conversation, Richard had not given me any indication as to why Dave Pearce wanted to see me. At 4:30 there was a phone call from Richard, informing me both he and Dave were running behind schedule and that we would have to meet at the Sarn Services just up the road outside Bridgend on the M4 at about 5:30 pm.

I got into my car and made my way to the Sarn services a few miles along the M4 motorway and once again waited nervously in the cafeteria. Being alone, I did not have to indulge in idle chit chat, which suited me just fine, wishing to be alone with my dark, pessimistic thoughts, thoroughly convinced of the worse-case scenario. At about 5:45 both Richard Cooper and Dave Pearce finally appeared. Each bought a coffee, before slowly heading to where I sat. Despite having consumed a few cups of coffee that afternoon, my throat and mouth exhibited a dryness equivalent to that of the Sahara desert. Richard could see my apprehension and broke the silence by commenting,

'Don't worry, we're not going to sack you and there is nothing to worry about, but what we are about to tell you is in the strictest confidence.'

Dave then took over the conversation and began explaining why we were meeting away from the treatment plant. He began asking if I had made any specific arrangement to go away for the three weeks at Christmas. I told him I had no definite plans and it was just a chance to relax and chill out. He smiled, obviously pleased with my answer and continued.

'Good, because I am going to ask you to cancel your holidays. You will be a key person during to the shutdown of the plant ensuring all paperwork is completed properly The Council and Welsh Development Agency have just bought the plant and want us to vacate the site by the last day of January 1992. All wastes will have to be removed off site and treated elsewhere as there is no time to treat it all. Any good mineral oil on site will be sold and any waste such as those which Richard Mainwaring brought illegally to site will be shipped to Shanks at Bedford. All storage tanks will have to be cleaned gas tested and sold for scrap or used by any of the Hyperwaste sites this news has not yet been released officially so you cannot tell anyone, and especially Cedric.' Richard smiled and reiterated the statement, 'Yes, you DO NOT tell Cedric.' Deliberately emphasising the DO NOT.

'Do you have any questions?' they asked me.

'Well yes I do,' I replied. 'I have to use my 15 days holiday by the end of the year and I was told they could not be carried over. So what happens with those holidays?' Dave Pearce looked at me and smiled. Which was a bit disconcerting as he very rarely smiled, was I being placated before they eventually sacked me, I wondered?

'Don't worry you will not lose them, either you will get payment in lieu or we can carry some days over to next year's holiday it can be sorted without you losing out, I promise.'

'When can we start to get the wheels in motion I asked?'

'Well,' Richard replied thoughtfully, before continuing.

'We cannot tell anyone at the moment but you can start taking inventory of materials on site and sorting out any waste to be shipped off site for disposal. That can be done without involving anyone else and without arousing too much suspicion. Also you will not be helping any of the other depots from now on you will be committed 100 per cent to help close the treatment plant. You will stay on site permanently until the final closure. The only holidays from now until the end of January will be Christmas Day, Boxing Day and New Year's Day.

There were so many questions in my mind. 'What is to stay and what is to be removed?'

Dave answered that question, 'The only things to remain are the main offices and the vehicle workshop, every bit of pipe work and process tank is to be taken down and scrapped, including the boiler and boiler house. The old process building is to be completely knocked down. All new equipment is to be removed and either scrapped or sold including all new equipment.

On the drive home, that evening, my thoughts were in turmoil. What would happen after the closure of the facility? Both Dave Pearce and Richard assured me that I had a future with the Hyperwaste, but I did not fully believe them, especially when considering recent events within the company.

For the next week I had great difficulty in keeping the secret about the closure of the plant from both Jamie and Cedric. They knew I had been to a meeting with Dave and Richard away from the plant and kept enquiring about the content of the meeting. I managed to fob them off with some project Dave had been involved in and wanted my contribution. I felt bad about having to lie to Jamie, but not particularly Cedric.

I did not have to keep the secret for too long as events soon became public and broadcast on the local Television and printed in the local newspaper, the latter building up its part in the closure, claiming they had been the ones who had helped bring it about. Richard Cooper called us all into a meeting explaining the plant had to be completely wound up by the last day of January 1992 and then explained the programme by means of time lines for the next few weeks. All oils had to be emptied out of the tanks, which he estimated to be in the region of 600,000 gallons of waste oil. All tanks to be completely emptied and gas tested for oxygen, hydrogen sulphide, carbon monoxide, methane and flammables prior to being cleaned and broken up by the welders. The demolition company would not charge us for breaking up the plant, but would get all the proceeds after selling the scrap metal or reselling the process equipment, apart from the filter press, pumps and lime slaker, which would be put into storage until another location for a treatment plant could be found.

Enquiries were made about some part of Hyperwaste having the boiler, which thanks to Cedric remained in pristine condition, despite being in service for over seventeen years. My old friend John Willis and John Andrews even came down to have a look at it, but decided they did not want it at that time. After a large amount of enquiries and rejections, Dave Pearce gave it to the dismantling company to do with it as they wished. Then sod's law applied, within a week of the boiler being given to the dismantling company, a large job came up with the industrial division which required the use of a boiler and the output in heat would be just the ticket. Unfortunately the dismantling company now owned it and sold it back to Hyperwaste for a few thousand pounds. What a financial blunder!

The workload for all of us on plant then grew exponentially and the complete antithesis of the previous two years, from doing virtually nothing to there not being enough hours in the day to complete the work, such as, carrying out inventories for all the waste paints and other materials which Richard Mainwaring had illegally dumped on us during his period as Area Sales Manager. The WDA section on the council, however helped with the paperwork, after all it was in their interest to ensure everything went as smoothly as possible and without any delays regarding the final winding up of the plant. They had to sort the area facility ready for the opening of the Garden Festival site at the end of May 1992.

The welding company contracted to dismantle the site, had quite a cavalier attitude towards their work, Jamie even saw one welder cutting a section of pipe work on which he decided to sit and the end fell to the ground with the welder following closely behind. Apparently, the welder landed on the ground, shook his head and carried on cutting another section of pipe. Thankfully he did not hurt himself too much. Richard had ultimate responsibility for the site, when he heard about the incident, he went ballistic, unusual for the normally placid Mr Cooper and tore the contractors off a strip, ensuring all safety procedures were adhered to before they carried on working.

Hyperwaste tankers arrived in convoy, taking the waste oils to other treatment plants for disposal, lower rates had been negotiated by Richard and Dave Pearce.

Cedric was prone to getting in accidents like hoses uncoupling for some unknown reason and rancid dirty oily water being sprayed over him while it was being transferred to a 20 tonne tanker under pressure. Although I had my suspicions some of the tanker drivers somehow manufactured the incidents, particularly when it involved Cedric.

Gradually through the whole of December the oils were emptied from the storage tank, and as each had its oil removed, the demolition company moved in to disconnect all the pipe work, depending on the state of the tanks, some were broken up, while the good tanks were loaded on to vehicles taken to the company's storage depot for possible resale. As the plant was slowly dismembered, I felt sad, melancholy and somewhat depressed, all the past work which had been put into building and establishing the facility with all the thought planning and preparation mainly by Craig Theake and the contractors during their evenings spent in The County Hotel in the early seventies. With the dismembering complete, all that would be left of the plant would be a long lost distant memory. As each section of pipe work was cut, I felt my heart break. Recalling all the good times during my tenure at West Mercian Oil Refineries, as, unfortunately memories do tend to evoke, showing themselves mostly through rose tinted spectacles.

By the middle of January most of the process tanks and pipe work had been virtually removed, the boiler had been shipped to the northeast. Only the main refinery building was left. We had a bit of a fright when it was thought the lagging around the process tanks was asbestos, however it became evident that it was not asbestos, but another type of safer insulation.

Due to all the knocking about inside the old process building by the demolition contractors, alarms became dislodged and the slightest whiff of wind set them off. The first person on the contact list was Cedric, who, I later discovered, being hourly paid, received a minimum rate of four hour call out payment each time he went into the plant to either reset the alarms, or disconnect the particular section which had set off the alarm in the first place.

Eventually, the local police became fed up with having to wait for Cedric to travel all the way from Merthyr Tydfil, where he lived, instead, after perusing the list noticed a local telephone number, which unfortunately turned out to be mine. During January 1992, I began receiving late night calls virtually every night to reset the intruder alarms, which not only annoyed myself but also Cedric who missed out on his call out payment, which probably amounted to approximately £150 for a call out at least five times a week. He complained vociferously to Richard Cooper about his loss of earnings. I, on the other hand, being staff, received no payment whatsoever, which in truth

128

Richard did not mind, not having to pay me overtime. What he did mind was the continual ear bashing he received from Cedric and his dogmatic, opinionated attitude. At last, Richard decided the alarms would not be set at night to stop them going off at ungodly hours of the night and prevent personnel, mainly me, being called out to reset them which I was not too upset about, having no recompense for my troubles.

Two weeks before the deadline for the closure of the plant, we all had congregate in the main conference room, all of us uncertain as to why we needed to be there, however I should have realised from past experiences with other companies, when the workforce congregated for a meeting with higher management, it usually indicated bad omen, especially when we discovered it involved one to one meetings with Dave Pearce, the Hyperwaste hatchet man as we all knew from past experience.

The first to meet Dave Pearce were the garage personnel Phil, Jacob, Julian and the foreman Colin George. Of them all, only Julian, the apprentice lost his job and made redundant the others were told they would be based at the new depot being built on the outskirts of Cardiff, near Caerphilly and in the process of being constructed to replace the inadequate depot currently being used, which comprised of a small brick building which acted as the main office and a small compound with hard core surface and inadequate drainage which tended to be the parking area for the vehicles. Julian being made redundant came as no surprise. After all, his father had previously been the engineering director and had been pushed out during the bloodletting at boardroom level. All the other garage personnel would, following the closure of the plant, be based at the new depot near Cardiff, helping set up the garage facility for maintaining the vehicles.

The next to go in was Helen Jones, Richard's secretary, who was told there was no job for her at the new Depot. In any case, she had intended on moving to Sheffield and live with her boyfriend, so she was not too upset by the news.

It was my turn next and this time fully expecting the chop. My job title at that time was Plant Chemist, now with no plant, my job now appeared to be superfluous to requirements. Both Dave Pearce and Richard Cooper sat on the one side of the huge manager's desk in the plant manager's office. I sat apprehensively on the other side of the table, Dave spoke first.

'First let me thank you for all your work over the past few weeks and for the two years at the plant.

'Here we go.' I thought, *'here it comes, the "but" part.'*

Dave continued. 'We are transferring you to the new depot near Cardiff, where you will have a new job title. The one of Plant Chemist no longer applies, you will be called Technical Controller. You will have the pool car, the Escort as your company car. Your job will be to become   acquainted   with   the   new   legislation concerning the transportation of hazardous waste due to come into effect next year, you will do as you have been doing advise the depots on the type of transport to use for shipping waste and also carry out any analysis using the laboratory equipment as before.'

At this point, Richard interrupted, with a hint of a smile on his face.

'Excuse me Dave, you haven't asked Vinson if he wants the job.'

I tried not to appear too eager, but in all probability did not contain my relief at having a job

'Yes I will take it,' I replied, trying desperately to curtail my relief and eagerness.

Dave continued 'Good, glad to hear it, you will also do work for the depots when required, also I want you to set up a documentation system similar to the one we had in my previous company which sets out clearly how waste is to be shipped and the safety equipment to be used, but we will sort all that out when the laboratory is moved down to the new depot. Hyperwaste still intends to set up a treatment plant somewhere in the South Wales area but that is for the future. All I have to say to you is you still have a job and not to worry.'

The meeting ended shortly afterwards and I left the office relieved at the unexpected outcome.

Unhappily, the outcome for Jamie was the total opposite and he was told he would have to finish when the plant closed and the same applied to Cedric. I did feel guilty at still having a job when Jamie would be unemployed. Cedric had reached 64 years of age, so his pension would kick in shortly so it was no hardship for him, although he was pissed off at not being offered a job, considering it an affront to his skills.

During the last couple of weeks we worked flat out trying to get the designated tasks completed before the end of last day of January. As I worked in the laboratory, packing equipment and chemicals away for shipment to the new site on the outskirts of Cardiff, one particular day I heard a loud scream and a thud coming from the toilets which had a small connection between the toilet in the main office block and the portacabin which we used as the main canteen. I went to investigate only to be met by Jacob, one of the mechanics from the garage supporting a slightly dazed Cedric, with his left arm hanging around Jacob's neck as he hobbled on his left leg. He looked a comical figure, with his overalls covered in dust, dishevelled hair and glasses hanging at an acute angle on his nose.

131

Now if it had been anyone else, I would have been sympathetic. Upon questioning Jacob about what had transpired, he replied moving his head indicating he was actually referring to Cedric and at the same time desperately trying to hold back from bursting out laughing.

'He was disconnecting the joining corridor between the office block and the portacabin and fell through the ceiling, fortunately I was in the toilet when it took place and found him on the floor.'

Cedric could be such an odious person and generally unsympathetic individual on occasions, I found the incident quite funny and knew if it had been someone else in that situation, then Cedric would have shown no sympathy towards them telling them they were 'a stupid fucker' or other such terms of endearment and sympathy.

Both Jacob and I looked at each other, both of us desperately trying not to burst out in unrestrained laughter. I did not know what to say and asked more crass questions about the incident. Cedric being too dazed to reply so Jacob became his spokesperson, all the time trying to stifle his desired intention to burst out in unrestrained laughter while relating the story.

I asked Cedric where he hurt to which he replied croakily, 'My back and left leg both hurt.' I could see Jacob looking away desperately trying to contain himself and not 'lose it' in front of Cedric.

The reader must think us both uncaring and heartless, callous individuals, but Cedric tended to be such an obnoxious person, it in no way appeared cruel to us, mainly because of his personality. I also remembered what Cedric called the welder following his rapid descent from the pipe-work, a few weeks earlier which was far from complimentary.

We took Cedric into the laboratory office. I then searched for the first aid kit to patch up any cuts and bruises on Cedric's old body. When Jamie came into the laboratory, seeing the state of Cedric and hearing the story, he too had enormous difficulty in restraining himself from unbridled laughter.

Jacob and I were alone together after Cedric had returned to his office. It was then we both laughed out loudly commenting how we were both looking at each other when Cedric looked dishevelled and we trying not to laugh after seeing the bemused expression on the maintenance engineer's face.

Although Richard tore the demolition company apart for the accident with their welder, he did not say a word to Cedric. Jamie tended to be more cynical about the whole incident, believing it had been set up by Cedric in the hope of claiming compensation for an industrial accident, prognosticating he would later play on his back problems directly attributing them to the fall.

The final weeks of the plant approached and I began to get maudlin about the final demise and closure of the site. This feeling of depression was heightened when Richard Cooper began going through some ancient documentation relating to the plant and discovered some old photographs of the founding fathers of West Mercian Oil Refineries, namely Phil Meredith and Craig Theake. One photograph showed them standing together smiling, full of ambition and hope. My God, they all looked so young with their DA haircuts and drainpipe trousers and suits. I remembered, during the early days of WMO, occurred while I was still in my early twenties and a naive, young graduate when I knew them. Now I was middle aged and in my early forties, my perception of them amended because of those passing years, they were only youngsters.

133

During those last days of the plant, I could not resist winding Cedric up just one last time. One afternoon I observed a driver of a rather large articulated vehicle gesticulating to Richard Cooper, obviously enquiring whether he could turn his vehicle in the plant instead of having to resort to a complicated turning manoeuvre. The driver nodded which indicated Richard had obviously given the permission required. The vehicle drove into the plant and drove past the boiler house where Cedric lurked and sat in wait for any event on which he could pounce.

The vehicle then drove clockwise around the area where the storage tanks had previously been located drove past the car park and out through the main gates.

Almost immediately, I observed Cedric, emerging from his lair.

'Let's have some fun with Cedric.' I said to Helen.

'Oh, no Vinson!' she said, almost begging for me not to do anything. I then went to laboratory door and looked across at Cedric, trying to give my most indignant facial appearance.

'Did you see that vehicle from the Garden festival driving through? It's not right Cedric, suppose he knocked one of the cars, would we be insured, someone ought to say something to Rob '

'You're right,' replied Cedric angrily, 'I'm going to look for Richard and complain.' Before he could find Richard, I thought it only fair to warn my boss about the forthcoming maelstrom. When I did find him I enquired innocently, although I already knowing his answer.

'Who gave that driver permission to turn his vehicle on our site?'

'I did,' replied Richard indignantly as if I questioned his authority.

'I know,' I replied, 'but Cedric doesn't and he's on his way to put his point of view, sorry but I may have added fuel to the fire somewhat.'

Richard looked at me knowing full well the consequences, becoming embroiled in a one sided debate with Cedric about allowing vehicles permission to use the facility for turning.

He had enough on his plate without having to deal with an irate Cedric shouting at him like a banshee.

'Gee thanks mate.' With that, he put on his jacket. 'If he asks for me, tell him I had to go and visit a customer.' He shot out of the office and immediately disappeared. Such was the effect Cedric had upon people.

Wednesday 29th January arrived with Thursday and Friday, left in which to complete the work and close the plant. It was going to be tight but it looked as if we would have the plant ready for the hand over by 5 pm on Friday, 31st January.

I was completing loading the last of the laboratory equipment and chemicals onto the vehicle for shipment down to the new site. I can't recall where Richard was, all I knew was that he was not on site that particular Wednesday morning. Mid-morning Helen called me, 'I have Richard on the line, he wants to talk to you urgently, there's a problem.'

I took the phone which she proffered. 'Hi Richard, what's the problem?'

'I have some bad news,' he replied. 'You know we thought we had until Friday to shut the plant? Well, it appears the lawyers have cocked up and thought there were only thirty days in January. The closure of the plant is set for tomorrow the 30th January which is what they have put on the agreement... they should have put the 31st. They told the Hyperwaste Board, the plant would close on the last day of the month. We have to be out by then, otherwise there is a huge penalty fee on, the terms agreed. So we have to be out by the 5:00 pm on the 30th Can we do it?' he asked.

'It will be tight but I think we can,' I replied.

'We have to,' he replied, adding, 'I will be in later today.'

I put down the phone and could not believe what had transpired. Our lawyers, ostensibly the cream of the intelligentsia in society could not get the amount of days in January correct. I called everyone together and explained the facts. Of course Cedric went *off on one* and went to call Richard on his mobile. That night we all worked extra hours trying to ensure everything would be completed by 5 pm Thursday, not Friday as previously thought.

Luckily, we had almost completed the closure beforehand, so by Thursday afternoon at 15.00, everything was done and our task complete. We all sat on the floor in the main conference room, exhausted, the office was devoid of any furniture, with only the carpets left to give some comfort to our posteriors. We could not even make a cup of tea or coffee. Richard went out and bought some wine with plastic cups enabling us to have a drink for the last toast and final farewell to the plant.

I was thoroughly depressed. I had been employed at the plant since its early days. I had left, returned and now here I was again at its demise. As with all endings, we reminisced about the early days of WMO and of Hyperwaste, recalling events and characters, both laughing and crying during the recollections. Only the main office block and garage remained from the old treatment plant. All the pipe work, tanks, the main process building effluent plant, the huge expensive clarifier and other pieces sold as they were. Large pieces of equipment, such as the lime slaker, filter press with its huge pumps and ancillary equipment put into storage, ready for the possibility of acquiring a new treatment plant. It was a sad and ignominious end to a wonderful oil refinery.

Finally, Richard made a short speech in which he thanked us all for our efforts over the past two and a half years, especially the last weeks ensuring the closure and transfer of the site went well and to plan. He explained his personal sadness at not being able to employ everybody after the closure and wished everyone well. He then told us we could all go, explaining he had to lock up and ensure the keys to the main gate, office building and garage were in the local council offices before the deadline of 5 pm. He, no doubt, wished to spend some time alone in the old refinery reminiscing about his time there, deep in his own secret thoughts.

Despite asking repeatedly, I never really discovered the amount of payment Hyperwaste received for selling the Treatment plant originally built by WMO. I am uncertain as to who actual knew, undoubtedly, Tom Driscoll and the other Directors knew. The company originally spent £250,000 in acquiring the site from West Mercian Oil, then forked out a further £600,000 for modifications and improved the plant to treat soluble oils, acids and alkalis, plus lawyers' and consultants' fees. So the price had to be at least £1 million for the sale in order to break even.

I do know however, for the financial year prior to the sale. Hyperwaste made a substantial loss of £500,000 for the year and were in the red and experiencing difficulty paying creditors, having to go cap in hand to the main French company. However for the following financial year, after the sale of the plant, the company made a profit in the region of £9 million and during the following years, able to expand and assimilate some of its competitors into the fold. It seems too much of a coincidence for the company to suddenly be making that much profit in one year, especially considering their previous circumstances.

Hyperwaste were unusually reticent in declaring how much they benefited financially out of the whole business venture, after selling to the council and the WDA. At the opposite end of the spectrum, the new owners of the facility were equally embarrassed at how much they had to pay the company to get them out of their hair, equally as reticent to divulge the actual amount. There can be no doubt, the amount was certainly not insubstantial.

Apart from Hyperwaste, there were other winners. The Garden Festival for 1992 which, despite all the problems went ahead, proving to be a minor success. It did, however, turn out to be the last one held.

After the festival, the surrounding ground which had been cleared and decontaminated of toxic material generated by the steelworks, thanks to the grant for the festival, gave birth to new private housing and a shopping development. No doubt, some dubious characters, previously mentioned, benefited financially and quite substantially from these developments.

CHAPTER 12

*T*he early days based at the new depot tended to be a bit unusual with the actual disposal operations for the depot still being run from the old office about two miles away.

During those first couple of weeks, with the new building being erected, it did not possess the main basic utilities, including telephone lines. I had not been issued with a mobile phone by the company, which I found slightly confusing considering my alleged position as 'technical guru' for the company. Although I did have my own personal mobile phone, I kept the number a strict secret only divulging it to close friends, having no wish to receive phone calls concerning work at ungodly hours of the night. The guys in the garage began setting the garage unit to their requirements while I commenced setting up the laboratory in a small side room which I had been allocated.

Having no mobile phone and there being no landline going to the facility, I was, to all intents and purposes, incommunicado with the rest of the Hyperwaste operations throughout the country. Bloody fantastic, if people wanted to get in touch with me they had to go through the old office, still the hub of the operation and contact Ryan Rhys the Depot Manager. Any messages to be relayed meant he had to get in his car and travel to the new site in order to pass them on. This process tended to be infrequent, as Ryan Rhys, for reasons, known only to him, exhibited a great reluctance to leave the sanctuary of his office, only doing so when absolutely necessary. This temporary state of being incommunicado allowed me time, without diversion or hindrance, to yet again, set up the laboratory in the small room, which I had been assigned. I had become quite used to installing the laboratory, having done it for the treatment plant in addition, taking the atomic absorption to various sites for on-site analysis. The hardest part required setting up the fume cupboard for extraction of any toxic fumes. Those first couple of weeks allowed me to relax and concentrate on setting up the laboratory during the day then without the additional distractions. Memories of the radio continually blaring out the record by Crowded House of '*Always take the weather with you*,' it seemed quite apt for the weather, at the time which, as I recall, tended to be mild and sunny. During the evenings at home with Stella, I felt quite tranquil and stress free.

Meanwhile Colin, Jacob and Phil, together with a new fitter, set up the workshop for maintaining the vehicles. Alastair Lawson, because of his accident had to finish working for the company and go on long term sickness, after which he eventually moved back to Scotland. During this time, I became friendly with the guys, having not really spent too much time with them during our short time together at the treatment plant. Often, I had lunch with them in their new small canteen with the usual banter and this is when we all got to know each other. Yes those too were good days. Unfortunately this utopian working life became short lived as one by one the utilities began to be installed at the site, electricity, gas heating, water and finally, the scourge of modern day society the telephone.

The offices on the upper floor slowly began taking shape with plush carpets being installed, finally after about a month, the office staff from the existing, old office began moving into the new building and the vehicles for the depot began being parked in the new compound, with this influx of staff so ended my

140

relatively tranquil existence. I realized my peaceful existence was at an end.

Slowly, bit by bit, when the transport depots throughout the UK discovered I could now be contacted, they began bombarding me with questions and my workload began to increase. Dave Pearce began appearing on the scene and insisting I became more involved with setting up his desired Technical Advice Document system. A system for all the drivers ensuring they had the correct tanker barrel for carrying the specific waste, also the correct TREM (Transport Emergency) cards with the correct hazchem boards for the vehicle together with the correct PPE and any other information which the driver should require specific to the particular job. I also became involved in setting up a new labelling software system for printing labels for drums. The waste regulations were at this time changing at a terrific rate. Whereas previously there were about 17 types of generic labels for waste known as the seven thousand series. In the early nineties this all altered and UN numbers had to be used for each waste in barrels, using the most concentrated or highly dangerous chemical contained in the specific barrel. For this I had the UN book, the gospel concerning waste, which contained approximately 3000 waste codes to choose, from which I had to choose the most relevant and specific identification for any drummed waste being transported, I then had to print them out and send them to the depots before the designated shipment date. As time went by, it became evident some generic labels could be used and so to reduce costs these generic labels were printed out in large quantities by printers and sent to the depots.

Dave Pearce loved computers and a wizard with any new software systems. Hyperwaste invested in a new software system for printing the labels. After first attending a seminar given by the company supplying the programme, Dave thought it best I should be away from the facility at the new depot and avoid any distractions. He suggested we go through the software package together at his home in Leicester.

Arriving at his house, it came as no surprise to discover his residence to be rather impressive and imposing in what seemed to be an extremely exclusive area of Leicester. What did come as a surprise to me was the amount of children Dave had, six altogether, all relatively young. Dave never seemed to be at home during his time with the company and forever staying in Manchester where the head office was to be located. Or alternatively, travelling the length and breadth of the UK visiting the various depots. He was an out an out workaholic. How he found time to procreate with his extremely attractive wife was beyond me. Also, the way in which Dave behaved towards his children, a loving doting father, completely belied his image within the company as the hatchet man, as if he had an alter ego. Upon reflection, the reason he worked so hard was to be a good provider for his family, which he obviously adored.

His wife made lunch for us and I spent all day going through the software system, discovering various deficiencies within the system, which the company promised to rectify. They had supplied the software to a number of other waste disposal companies and held another seminar in which all present discussed the problems and shortcomings and whether they could be resolved in the programme. I must confess Dave was a great help in setting up the programme helping to resolve the teething problems with the system, which he reported back to the supplier.

After I had been at the new facility for a few months, everyone from the old, existing office began moving into the new plush buildings. Richard Cooper based himself at Port Talbot taking care of the Industrial Division. Ryan Rhys became in charge of the site and worked until 7 most evenings.

While I was at the former treatment plant, Richard Cooper always insisted I finished at 4:30. At the new Depot, I continued with this habit, after all they were my agreed hours. Ryan resented the fact I left at 4:30 my normal hours although in charge of the depot, I did not come under his jurisdiction, instead reporting directly to Dave. It came to a head one evening when Dave Pearce tried to contact me at 5:15, to be informed by Ryan that I had left at 4.30 and in fact left at that time every day, which did not please Dave.

A couple of days later, he came down to the depot and had meeting with me. He was alright about it and stated he knew I finished at 4.30 my hours and that Richard Cooper sanctioned it. There was now the 'but' in the next sentence, 'But things have changed and we need you work until at least 5:30 in case there are issues with some of the depots and as Technical Controller, we need you to be available.'

I just looked at him, my thoughts being '*Typical, you expect me to work longer hours without any benefits!*' Dave looked at me as if he knew what I was thinking.

'Of course, I realise this means you will be required to work longer hours. I have been looking at the various salaries. I think your salary is far too low to begin with, considering the duties we expect you to perform, therefore, I am giving you a 30% increase in salary with immediate effect and a brand new company car, an estate would be preferable to carry various types of equipment and reagents I am also giving you a company phone. I hope that all softens the blow a bit?'

143

I just looked at him dumbfounded and speechless. I was appreciated after all. This was the man who had sacked numerous employees and here he was giving me a hefty increase in pay.

'Yes sure,' I blurted out as some sort of response.

'Good, I'm glad that is sorted out, so I can count on you to work until 5:30 or later if required from now on?'

'Yes, I understand,' I replied. With that we concluded the meeting. It was then I realised the company must have received quite a bit of money for the treatment plant.

True to his word, Dave immediately increased my salary by 30% and within a few weeks, I received a brand new top of the range Ford escort estate turbo diesel in racing green, a far cry from the clapped out reject vehicles I normally received up until that time. Things were definitely looking up.

Dave Pearce had a bad reputation within the company as the hatchet man, and of giving some of the depot managers such as Ryan and Ioan a rough time, but he always took care of me and as I recall never did me any harm career wise.

Dave was correct, my duties altered dramatically, and it was my task to ensure the drivers throughout the UK had the correct Technical advice documents for carrying hazardous materials. Also drums correctly labelled with the proper descriptions. The Hazardous waste legislation laws were changing at a fast pace and it was part of my duties to interpret the new laws and make certain the company complied. Also white papers were being issued to once again amend the Hazardous waste laws, and committees set up with personnel from the various waste disposal companies to discuss the proposed changes to the law, the implications and possible ramifications. I had to attend theses committee meetings and discuss any amendments we would like included in the white paper. I still had become involved in Chemical Cleaning projects for Middlesborough and also, doing inventories for drummed waste, ensuring the correct labelling was put onto the drums. My duties were so varied. As I try to recollect those days, I find it extremely difficult becoming involved with so many aspects of the waste industry at that time. Yet despite all these requirements in my duties, I found the job stimulating and enjoyable, most certainly varied but never, never boring.

After the depot had been open for a couple of months, it was decided to have an official opening inviting local dignitaries to publicise the event and promote the company. I still had my little laboratory in which to do the occasional analysis of the wastes, but by now, most of the wastes from the regular companies had been well documented and the toxic components known and quantified to the correct standards.

I had my little laboratory set up, with stirrers going agitating various conical flasks with coloured solutions of various sorts, all very impressive I thought. Dave brought in one of the local dignitaries and showed him the lab but I did not know him residing in a different area. The person asked a lot of questions concerning the analysis, my duties etc. Before he left I asked his name, he appeared quite miffed I did not know him. Like all politicians, I guess, slightly conceited.

'I'm Ron Davies the local MP,' he replied. Of course he later became Welsh Secretary after the 1997 election before falling ignominiously from grace after his '*moment of madness*' on Clapham Common, never making first Minister for Wales, the position he coveted the most.

My duties allowed me to extensively travel the country and meeting various people. I also became involved in other duties such as Land reclamations.

CHAPTER 13

I have to admit, the waste industry appeared to have more than its fair share of rogues, which is quite an indictment considering my previous experiences within the hi-tech industry which also had a overabundance of somewhat dubious characters, causing me to divert my career path, as a consequence of their, illegal, fraudulent behaviour at board room level. Although, returning to the subject of the waste industry, it has in recent times, become more tightly regulated and more professional in its outlook and behaviour.

In the case of Hyperwaste, to begin with, the company had Dave Moreland, your loveable Arthur Daley type spiv who enhanced his street-wise, fly-boy image by driving around in a Porsche 911 Turbo. It was alleged Dave had some sort of scam going on in one of the local steelworks involving the double booking of scrap lorries and being paid twice for waste loads by British Steel. Although the scam was all conjecture and never proven or verified. He was also involved in a well-known sexual liaison with the wife of the Managing Director of a waste consultant company which had been advising Hyperwaste on its forthcoming litigious battle with the Welsh Development Authority and local council. Tom Driscoll tried in vain to order, persuade, coax and generally cajole the flamboyant Dave into replacing his Porsche 911 with a car not quite so flamboyant or ostentatious and more in keeping with that of a company director, such as a top of the range Granada, Vectra or Lexus. Yet, despite Tom Driscoll's continued insistence and protestations, Dave hung onto his beloved Porsche 911. When Hyperwaste, or to be more accurate, Tom Driscoll, pushed him from the company, as part of the final termination agreement, Dave kept his treasured German engineered and manufactured sports car.

Another rogue within the company was Richard Mainwaring who exaggerated his qualifications, stating he had studied Chemistry at Cambridge. The most definite implication being he had studied at one of the prestigious universities within that city. He had indeed studied Chemistry in Cambridge but at the local polytechnic, where he obtained a HND and not a degree and not in a university as he often alluded. The *'Jeffrey Archer syndrome,'* as it is often known. He also had *'business'* dealings over in Southern Ireland involving a dubious waste company based there. Richard insisted we accepted a load of waste material at the treatment plant, which the facility was not authorised to take, consisting mostly of paints and solvents. Richard Mainwaring overruled all of Richard Cooper's and my objections on the subject, saying we could put down on the paperwork, as intending to be used for *'tarting up'* the facility. That is to say, the waste was not to be disposed of but re-used. Although in reality most of the paints were well past their sell-by dates, with most having congealed or solidified in the pots due to the oxidation and ageing processes. All Richard Mainwaring was concerned about was being paid handsomely for taking the waste from the producer and basically fly-tipping at the treatment plant's expense.

Then, finally, the *piece de resistance* the company had Ryan Rhys, the Depot Manager at the Cardiff depot who had all sorts of frauds and scams going on, together with a very liberal and rather extremely broad, interpretation of the hazardous waste laws, frequently landing him in hot water as he pushed his particular reading of the those laws to the limit.

Ryan possessed the ability to react with unerringly sharp responsiveness, particularly when cornered or unexpectedly caught off guard. I recall standing in the office one morning as Ryan received a telephone call from a particularly irate customer. The customer had not received the 20 cubic metre, roll-on-roll off skip he had been expecting to be delivered to his site that very morning. It was obvious from his expression, Ryan had forgotten to schedule delivery of the large skip to the premises. Straight away, like a flash of lightening, he came up with a reply.

'Could you hang on a minute?' he asked the annoyed customer, 'While I try to contact the driver on the radio. I will have to put you on hold is that alright?'

With that, he pressed the 'secrecy' button on the phone and then nonchalantly carried on with his paperwork as if he had not a care in the world. After what he considered to be a reasonable amount of time, Ryan picked up the redundant phone and returned to his conversation with the waiting customer.

'I'm sorry,' he informed the person on the other end, while lying shamelessly through his teeth, although, at the same time, managing to exude a mixed impression of innocence and concern.

'It appears the vehicle has had one of the tyres blow out and is stuck on the hard shoulder of the motorway. The driver has contacted the tyre company and is waiting for them to replace it. Can we re-schedule the skip for tomorrow, as we have no other vehicle available at the moment?'

The customer must have uttered some oaths on the other end of the line, but agreed to Paul's fraudulent request. Ryan put the phone down and smiled to himself before announcing proudly to everyone in the office, obviously elated at the fact he had once again managed to extricate himself out of another predicament.

'That was a close one.'

He must have had a list of tried and trusted lies memorized in his repertoire which he worked through in rotation.

Another instance, the office was extremely busy, with phones ringing incessantly. I picked up one of the phones only to get an enraged woman on the other end. Memories of my days working in the Customer Liaison Department of Birchwater came flooding back. I am not bragging when I say this, but I do have the ability to placate people on the phone and have a reasonable telephone manner, a legacy from my previous employment at Birchwater, particularly when it comes to women, with the ability to flirt outrageously with the fairer sex via the phone I possess the type of face and physique suitable for enticing telephone conversations only. After finally managing to calm down, the woman began explaining she had ordered a tanker to collect her septic tank waste, and had apparently informed Ryan, the tanker required 100 feet of hose as the effluent tank was a considerable way from the main road. On the first day the tanker turned up, with only 40 feet of hose, totally inadequate for the required task. The woman contacted the office and once again talked to Ryan concerning the job which necessitated putting postponing it for another day. On the second day and the tanker still had an insufficient length of suction hose and, yet again, the collection had to be postponed. This was now the third attempt with the collection and scheduled for 9:30 that morning. It was 12:00, and still no sign of the tanker. The woman considered she had been told a falsehood, yet again, judging Ryan, as a result of her dealings with him, to be a mendacious, compulsive liar and a thoroughly untrustworthy individual. I had a terrible job convincing her to put the phone down and that I would indeed phone her back with an answer. She was not happy at that, considering the office to be full of duplicitous characters. Eventually, she agreed to my request, putting the phone down and waited for me to phone her back. After asking team in the office, I discovered the tanker was scheduled for that morning with the requested 120 ft of hose. Sheila the office manageress contacted the driver and informing me the vehicle was about 30 minutes away from the house. When I tried to phone her back, I discovered her line to be engaged and remained so for well over half an hour. When I did eventually get through, the woman answered the phone, I detect her feeling of euphoria down the line, especially after informing her that the tanker was on its way.

'I know,' she replied with unreserved enthusiasm.

'It arrived 5 minutes ago and he has all the correct equipment, thank you very much. At least you are not an inveterate liar like Ryan Rhys. What is your name?'She then enquired. After I told her, she added, 'Next time I will ask for you Vinson.' For some inexplicable reason she associated me with arranging to get the tanker there and performing miracles in that short period of time, although, in truth, all I did was answer her question. Still it was nice to get the credit and discover what some of the customers thought of the depot Manager.

Yet, somehow, despite all their peccadilloes, it was hard to dislike all these characters mentioned as they exuded personal charm and charisma as most people of shady and duplicitous character tend to do. Those charismatic attributes, helped mitigate their indiscretions somewhat, as one could not intensely dislike them.

151

Another infamous episode concerning Ryan arose involving another dubious character named Alf Waters, one of the drivers. Alf returned to the depot late one Friday evening with a full load of sceptic tank sludge on his vehicle. With his persuasive and somewhat overbearing, dogmatic manner, Alf casually suggested to Ryan, with it being so late in the day, rather than take the sceptic tank effluent to the nearest authorised Welsh Water treatment plant, located quite a few miles away, perhaps he could discharge the contents of his tanker down the nearest drain access point located slap bang in the middle of the parking lot of the yard. Ryan could be easily coerced, or perhaps bullied would be a better description, by some of the more overpowering, opinionated drivers, of which Alf was most indubitably one.

So, with Ryan's authority, Alf began connecting the three inch polypropylene pipes to the outlet valve of the tanker, putting the open end of the pipe into the drain. After completing the setting-up exercise, Alf opened the main valve on the tanker and discharged its vile smelling contents down the open receptacle. After illegally discharging the effluent, both Ryan and Alf finished their work for the day, and went home for the evening. In both cases, home could be classified as any number of locations within the area, for in addition to having liberal interpretation on the disposal of hazardous waste, both had fairly liberal versions and understanding on the vows concerning marriage and fidelity. Both Ryan and Alf had wives, but indulged in numerous extra marital affairs whenever or wherever the opportunity arose, which appeared to be quite often in both cases.

That evening the consequence of their illegal action had disastrous results and ramifications, not involving the regulatory authorities, but individuals far more sinister and dangerous, with alleged associations to organised crime.

Unluckily, the drain outlet from the Hyperwaste yard meandered directly under a prestigious, large, popular nightclub situated next to the depot. The night club now, no longer exists, having been closed for some years and the building demolished. It had been rumoured the club had strong links with organised crime. However, whether this transpired to be the case or not, the Manager of the night club in question was a formidable, frightening person in his own right. A person constantly attired in, black suits, fedora, heavily tinted sunglasses, white tie and dark shirts. He also happened to be extremely stockily built and looked, as if, in his younger days could have had gone ten rounds with Mohammed Ali and during the tournament, given the latter a 'run for his money.' He had all the attributes of a pugilist, exhibiting a broken nose and cauliflower ears, all of which completed this rather intimidating picture. He could easily have passed for one of the Blues Brothers.

On the night of the illegal dumping, the nightclub had a huge entertainment night planned, with some high profile artistes booked to perform. The place was a sell out and bursting at the seams, with the management expecting an extremely busy, highly profitable, lucrative evening. That is, until Ryan and Alf performed their disappearing trick with 10 tonnes of highly odorous, pungent sewage waste.

This particular load of sewage waste managed to be quite overpowering, having been fermenting in its container for an extensive period of time, somewhere on the rural outskirts of Cowbridge. Because of its extended gestation period, the sceptic waste exuded somewhat obnoxious odours, odours which unfortunately, managed to permeate through the

153

ventilation system of the night club, with the vile, disgusting odour eventually managing to pervade, not only the main hall, but every nook and cranny of the premises. The result being the customers could not tolerate the smell and had to evacuate the building. It was quite some time before the smell began to abate which also necessitated copious amounts of disinfectant and expensive fragrances being profusely dispersed throughout the nightclub.

To quell any complaints from their customers the manager considered it prudent to offer free drinks and some sort of compensation for the night's debacle. What should have been a financial success turned into a financial calamity, with very little or possibly no profit being made in the venture.

That same evening the manager went around to the depot with some colleagues to have a 'discussion' with Mr. Rhys. However, by this time fortunately for them, both Ryan and Alf had vacated the scene of the crime and no longer on the premises.

The manager did not give up on his '*little discussion*' with Ryan and appeared at the office on the Monday morning. Fortunately for Ryan, having had a few meetings with the manager, he knew what he looked like and quickly hid when he saw the imposing figure approaching the small building risibly referred to as '*the depot.*'

News spread quickly throughout the locality about evening's fiasco at the club and so Ryan quickly became aware of disastrous events and knew exactly what had caused them, although he would never admit to it. Nevertheless, he had no intention of being confronted by the leviathan in black, hiding behind the door in the small kitchen after giving his staff brief but explicit instructions for them to indicate they had no knowledge of his whereabouts.

After that, Ryan kept away from the depot as much as possible during the next couple of weeks to avoid any confrontation with the manager, who, fortunately gave up in his quest as he had no real proof Ryan was responsible or knew of the discharge, although he harboured deep suspicions about the night's events and Ryan's involvement.

There was another manager in the Welsh area, Ioan Davies. Both he and Ryan had started work with Pembroke Sludge and had worked together for a number of years. Ioan too had his frauds and little earners but was of a highly nervous disposition. Whereas Ryan had the ability to blatantly brazen out any misdemeanours and joke his way out of a situation, Ioan was not such an inveterate liar and considerably more serious in temperament with a short fuse.

Ioan had a drink problem. One of the depot managers Calvin Maynard was visiting the West Wales depot and paying a courtesy call as he was in the area. Ioan had recently acquired a super duper hands free phone with what the Americans termed a squawk box and while Calvin was in the office, Ioan decided to show off his new acquisition when it rang, he put it on loudspeaker. It was the depot foreman on the other end.

'Hi Ioan, it's Mike here, they have no Teachers in the off licence, will Bells whisky be okay?'

Everyone knew of his addiction to the dreaded firewater as Ioan and his wife would drink a bottle of wine between them every evening together with a number of shorts, mostly whisky. Ioan also chain-smoked. The combination of the two plus the stress of the job and trying to hide the little sidelines would eventually prove too much for Ioan a few years after I joined Hyperwaste had a massive heart attack.

Dave Pearce, the infamous hatchet man had become the area director for South Wales. It had been rumoured Dave had left his previous company under a cloud, having been implicated in some fraudulent activity in the company. Although never substantiated. But it was always believed Dave was put in as director by Tom Driscoll, because of nefarious activities. It was your typical poacher turned gamekeeper scenario. Dave knew all the tricks and scams and could not be bamboozled in any way when it came to concealing nefarious activities.

Dave kept a tight rein on both Ryan and Ioan giving them both a rough time about their amount of business they brought in each month. Whenever Dave Pearce visited his depot, Ioan would become highly agitated, for days before, smoking and drinking more than usual.

It was time for the six monthly sales review to be held in Southampton. All the sales people and depot managers were to meet the night before, have an evening meal in the hotel and have the meeting the next day and travel back in the evening

The plan was Steve Houghton, one of the new managers, would drive from the depot, picking Ioan up. They would then drive to one of the services on the M4 outside Cardiff, where Ryan and Gerald Charters would park their vehicles and travel down to Southampton in Steve Houghton's car. This was supposed to all happen about 5 pm. Unfortunately, Ryan as usual, despite repeated telephone calls from Ioan, refused to leave the depot, always attending to urgent business. For some inexplicable reason this agitated Ioan even more than usual, despite Ryan being the main person responsible for them all being late at the hotel that evening. Eventually Ryan managed to get to the rendezvous by 6:30pm, almost an hour late. By which time Ioan was virtually bouncing around the car, he did not like to be kept waiting and had become extremely volatile.

Ryan was his usual self, trying to act all non-chalet, blasé self, although he too hated meetings with Dave. The four of them made their way down in Phil's car, Ioan and Gerald Charters sitting in the back.

Ioan began sweating profusely and still highly agitated. Gerald suggested they stop on the way for a coffee at one of the service stations on the M5 south and so Ioan could have a smoke to calm his nerves after which they resumed the journey south. They arrived at the hotel car park by which time Ioan began complaining about severe pains in his chest. As he got out of the car, he collapsed. Gerald performed CPR while the others phoned for an ambulance. The ambulance arrived within a few minutes. However, poor Ioan had sadly passed away despite all Gerald's valiant attempts to revive him. The doctors pronounced Ioan dead on arrival, at the local hospital.

The Sales meeting was cancelled, everyone returned home and with arrangements made to get Ioan's body back home to West Wales. Ryan never really forgave himself for causing Ioan to get distressed while waiting for him and believe Ryan still feels guilty to this day about the events of that day and his part in it. Although in reality, Ioan's death was only a matter of time due, to his lifestyle and the stress of the job, exacerbated by his dubious activities and because of the aforementioned circumstances, despite being in his late forties, Ioan appeared much older than his years and could easily have passed for someone in his sixties.

CHAPTER 14

I first met Karl Barclay when he visited the newly acquired WMO treatment plant. If my memory serves me correctly, it must have been around August 1989. He was normally based at the Cardiff depot and had worked for the company a number of years during the times when it had been known as 'Pembroke Sludge,' which as a company name never really appealed to me, verging on onomatopoeic, conjuring up images of thick, viscous, and brown, mud-like material. He remained with the company when it became assimilated into the Hyperwaste Empire. Karl was the foreman at the Cardiff Depot and Ryan's right hand man. Although Karl did all the 'hands-on work,' Ryan took all the credit when things went right, but, of course, Karl always being apportioned the blame when things went 'tits up,' which, I have to confess, as far as I can recollect, was quite rare. Karl 'led by example' always getting involved, utilising a method of leadership I admired then and still admire immensely to this day, as with Craig Theake the former Director of West Mercian Oil. Karl worked harder than any of the men working under him and he was most definitely not work-shy, despite being in his mid-fifties. He belonged to the *old school* as far as the work ethic was concerned. In addition, he possessed a wicked sense of humour, which was accompanied by an almost maniacal laugh, something akin to the old '*Carry On*' actor Sid James. We always indulged in a bit of work place banter, forever 'taking the Mickey' out of each other, but it was all in good fun with nothing malicious in it. I called him Alzheimer and he called me Doc.

158

During the intervening years, he frequently visited the treatment plant, but I only became really friendly and got to know him whilst based at the new depot site following the closure of the treatment plant.

Often I accompanied Karl on site visits for assessing work and the type of vehicles for specific projects and helping him to estimate overall costs. The first assessing job we both went on together was the British Airways maintenance facility based at Heathrow Airport which was closing down and required cleaning and the removal of oils and waste. Karl and I were given the task of visiting the site and the remit of putting together a quote for the project.

We met the site agent, who was hoping to sell or rent out the large facility, but he first had to arrange removal and disposal of any remaining chemicals on the site and then arrange the cleaning and removal of the superfluous storage tanks. He appeared to be your stereotypical agent, attired in an expensive pin striped suite, exuding an air of confidence, speaking with a refined English accent. Karl and I wore our working clothes, knowing full well the inspection would require us climbing and heaving ourselves into fairly inaccessible, grimy, heavily polluted locations.

We convened with the agent at the designated place, before being provided with security passes allowing access into the Heathrow site. The three of us walked around the facility and then Karl and I were shown the storage tanks, mostly containing fuel oil, and diesel, necessitating both emptying and cleaning. The job looked fairly standard. However during our walk about we came upon a large sump, which contained an obnoxious, foul-looking sludge. Almost immediately, I enquired if the site been utilised as an electroplating operation. The agent answered he thought it had, but was not fully certain of the fact. I had not brought any sample jars or testing kits for further investigation of the sludge, which could contain cyanide if the building had indeed been used for electroplating, my experience of copper electroplating gained at Cox & Sons coming to the fore.

Now all laymen think being given the designated title of 'Industrial Chemist,' you are able to look at an unknown material and by some uncanny, X-ray vision, possess the ability to tell them exactly what the material is and the concentrations of any toxic materials contained therein, as if the term Chemist suddenly instils you with mystical, magical powers. This agent was no exception. As I looked down into the sump containing the sludge, he asked me, 'What is it?' as if I was the font of all chemical knowledge.

I don't know what possessed me, but I looked up at him, and putting the tip of my forefinger to my thumb of my right hand made an 'o' then moved it back and forth slowly over my rather large protuberance on my face, namely my nose.

'Do you know what that means?' I asked in devilment while I persisted in moving my thumb and forefinger up and down my nose.

He looked at me slightly bemused. 'No,' he replied.

I then answered 'Fuck (k) no (w) se!' strongly emphasising the play on words. The agent looked at me, still perplexed. Karl appeared absolutely horrified, before looking away, shaking his head in disbelief at my attempted joke and the play on words accompanied by the hand gesture. Eventually the agent understood the joke and chuckled slightly, although the chuckle was probably more out of politeness than anything else. Karl meanwhile, still looked mortified.

'Oh I see,' replied the agent. I then told him if we got the project then we would take samples and assess what materials lay within the sump. After our survey of the site we left, and told the agent we would get back to him with a rough price for the project after discussing it with the depot manager.

All the while, Karl kept repeating over and over again throughout the car journey back to South Wales, 'Well you've lost us that little job. It would have been a nice little job too!!' I told him the guy thought the joke funny but Karl was convinced I had lost the possible contract.

It transpired after we had given the agent our quote, we did in fact get the job, much to Karl's incredulity and disbelief. The unknown material in the sump turned out to be Trichloroethylene a heavy, insoluble, non-flammable solvent the one from my old Midland Oil days. There was a layer of dirty water on top which masked any odours.

Another project required Karl and me to travel to Aberearon and Aberystwyth on the West Wales Coast, to package and bring back some chemicals which were being disposed of by the local council. The job necessitated an overnight stay, and so we had to find accommodation for the night. Karl would not entertain the thought of us spending more than £20 per night for us each. Although I told him the job had probably been budgeted at £50 each for accommodation and at any rate, the directors always ensured they stayed at the best hotels, so we were entitled to a little luxury. Still, he was adamant, we could not be extravagant with the expense account. Because of his intransigence, we continued searching the area for a place to stay for a considerable period of time. Eventually, we located a small B& B on the outskirts of Aberystwyth for the bargain basement price of £15 each per room per night.

I had to go in and ask all the details. Before I went back to the van to inform Karl the place had rooms and at a price agreeable to him, the landlady informed me she would not be cooking an evening meal because it was far too late. I informed her my colleague was a heavy drinker and would much rather prefer to go and have a meal in one of the local public houses with large amount of alcoholic beverages to choose from in order to feed his drinking addiction. The story was a complete fabrication as Karl only drank the occasional beer shandy and two of those would be his limit. Karl was most definitely not a drinking man which made the allegation all the more humorous. But I had to get my own back on him for the miles we had driven that evening looking for cheap accommodation. We both carried our overnight cases into the hotel and the landlady glared intimidating at Karl as he walked past her. Karl in turn glared back at the landlady.

As we climbed the stairway to our separate rooms Karl whispered to me, 'Does she know me, she gave me weird look?"

'How should I know if you have met her before, I don't know your life history?' before adding,

'Nah, that's probably her normal expression,' trying desperately not to smirk or laugh adding, 'It's just your imagination you know what these people from West Wales are like, mistrusting and deeply religious. Hell, damnation, fire and brimstone, the evils of the demon drink and all that.'

It appeared funny to me, being privy to how the woman now probably considered my colleague, a debauched, heavy drinker. It was his own fault for making me drive around Aberystwyth most of the evening, when I could have been in a nice, plush warm hotel room ages ago.

We went to the nearest pub that evening for steak and chips. I had a few pints, while Karl imbibed in his customary two pints of shandy, the beer being heavily laced with non-intoxicating lemonade.

That next morning while Karl and I tucked into our generous portions of breakfast, the landlady began chatting to us, informing us she was not from Aberystwyth, but in fact a native of the Welsh capital, Cardiff. Karl was always quite garrulous and chatted quite happily to her relaxing after their initial meeting. When during the conversation she suddenly informed Karl.

'I can tell you're not a drinker.' Karl looked at her with an evident bemused, perplexed expression on his craggy, well lived-in face.

'Sorry!' he exclaimed, 'I don't understand?'

'Well,' the landlady continued, while at the same time, pointing an accusing finger in my direction, 'your friend here said you had a drink problem. I can tell by looking and talking to you that's not true.'

I blushed slightly as Karl looked venomously in my direction, deliberately and silently mouthing the words, 'You bastard!' after first making certain the landlady could not see his lips. I could not help smiling despite being rumbled in my malicious slander concerning my colleague.

On the journey back to Caerphilly, all I heard was 'What a bastard you turned out to be.' Although said with 'a tongue in cheek' sort of attitude. To which I replied, 'Well I had to have my own back after you insisted on driving half way around West Wales looking for a place to stay for the night.' For years afterwards Karl and I would have a laugh about that trip on the west coast of Wales.

One winter afternoon during my time at the new depot, a sneak thief cheekily walked into the compound and drove off with one of the small company vans, in which somebody had left the keys. Karl got into his company vehicle with one of the fitters and set off in hot pursuit. As they drove down some country lanes,

Karl suddenly noticed what he thought was the stolen vehicle hidden amongst some trees just off the country lane. He stopped the van and quietly approached the van which appeared to be moving quite violently from side to side. Karl was under the erroneous impression that whoever had stolen the van was busily inspecting and sorting the tools out at the back of the van. Upon reaching it, Both Karl and the fitter opened the back doors of the small van only to catch a middle-aged couple immersed both physically and emotionally in coitus and completely oblivious to everything going on around them. When they came out of their sexual reverie, they were paradoxically embarrassed and angry. It quickly became evident to Karl it was not the van which had so recently been purloined from the depot. Karl and the fitter gave uttered some kind of apology before hastily vacating the area. Karl told me later, he believed the couple were indulging in an affair hence the reason for being in a relatively secluded area, well they considered it to be secluded until that evening.

As the years progressed we grew to respect each other and we found we disliked the same people such as Sir Andrew Chadrock Hulsey, a person we both disliked intensely along with multitudes of others. Karl was a company man through and through, always endeavouring to do the best he could when involved in projects, one of which was land reclamation in Dowlais Merthyr which the reader will hear about later on. He also became involved with the oil water treatment plant in Gwent, which unfortunately involved dealing with the double-dealing Sir Andrew Chadrock Hulsey, a person with whom the reader will eventually later become better acquainted.

CHAPTER 15

*R*ugby international day arrived, with Wales about to play their old adversary and arch-rival, England, at Cardiff Arms Park. It was the opening match of the Five Nations Rugby International Season. The previous season, England had been utterly victorious, convincingly defeating every team they had played against, in the process, winning, the Calcutta cup, Triple Crown, Championship and Grand Slam and elevating them to position of the favoured team, in repeating the previous year's performance, for the forthcoming new season. Most sports pundits fully anticipated the men in white would convincingly trounce Wales in this, their first confrontation of the new Five Nations calendar.

There are few things in life, if you happen to be Welsh, which compare with Rugby International Day in Cardiff, when Wales are playing whatever team. The capital city of Wales vibrant with colour, especially red, accompanied by a cacophony of noise and miscellaneous sounds, everyone excited at the prospect of the spectacular sports encounter ahead. The atmosphere is electric, particularly when inside the Rugby Stadium near the revered, hallowed turf, originally in the old Cardiff Arms Park, but since the beginning of the new century, in the new Millennium Stadium. I have been privileged to observe Wales playing in both grounds, experiences never to be forgotten. To be there amongst the throng, listening to the strains of traditional songs such as Calon Lan, Sospan Fach and of course, Cwm Rhondda, accompanied by contemporary songs such as *Delilah* or

Hymns and Arias reverberating inside the confines of the stadium. The whole atmosphere generates goose bumps along one's body, sending patriotic chills down the spine and also causing the fine hairs on the body to stand up, especially when Welsh voices ring out in unison singing the National anthem *Mae Hen Wlad Fy Nhadau (Land Of My Fathers)*. It is unbelievable, a cocoon of national pride covers the Principality, with not only those in the stadium, but the whole of Cambria enveloped in a great upheaval of patriotism, united as one in supporting their team in red, the modern day equivalent of Roman gladiators willing to put their bodies on the line for their country. The whole Celtic nation proclaiming, loudly, unashamedly and with pride, their heritage, roots, ancestry and of being Welsh.

For this particular occasion, as with all Welsh matches being played at the sacred ground in Cardiff, Hyperwaste hired a function room to entertain their esteemed and favoured customers in one of the prestigious Hotels located in the very heart of the Welsh capital. There had been a lot of '*blood spilled*' on the carpet at Hyperwaste boardroom level with quite a few of the Directors and managers suddenly and unexpectedly discovering themselves unemployed after being brutally culled by Tom Driscoll, the new Chief Executive Officer. Dave Pearce had now become Area Sales Director for the South, replacing Dave Moreland, his new promotion necessitated him, playing *Mien Host,* for the occasion, entertaining the esteemed customers. Being English, he attired himself in the England jersey encapsulating his fairly generous proportions and exhibiting his beer belly to great effect. The soiree was in full swing with buyers and people concerned with waste disposal from the big companies such as British Steel, SWEB, Alcoa, Alcan, Welsh

Water in the function room, consuming the alcohol available as if it the British government were about to suddenly introduce alcohol prohibition. Some of the customers went down to the watch the match at the Arms Park, whilst others remained in the warmth and comfort of the hospitality suite, with an excess of free food and drink close to hand and easily accessible.

Following the match, in which, joy of joys, despite being the underdogs, Wales beat England by one single point, helped by a spectacular Ieuan Evans try.... Hallelujah. All of Wales celebrated this momentous defeat of their old adversary with unabashed exuberance. One by one, after the match, the customers began slowly returning to the hotel function room from the rugby ground to finish consuming what little food and alcohol remained. Dave Pearce had, by this time, ingested quite a large amount of alcohol and thoroughly enjoying the atmosphere, despite his team losing by the one solitary point. Suddenly the diminutive form of Dave Moreland, the former Area Sales Director appeared in the doorway. Dave Moreland stood a mere 5ft 4inches in his stocking feet. In his right hand, he held a partly consumed glass of Brains beer. Some of the older, well-established clients acknowledged the former Director as he slowly walked into the room with a broad, alcoholic induced grin exuding on his slightly rotund face. The instant Dave Pearce saw the apparition of his rather miniscule predecessor, he approached him.

'I'm sorry Dave,' he began, his speech slightly slurred due to the large amount of alcohol coursing through his arteries and veins.

'But this is a Hyperwaste function, purely for Hyperwaste customers only. You no longer work for the company and are in fact a competitor, I am afraid I am going to have to ask you to leave!'

Almost immediately, without displaying any form of rancour or dissension, the former director obligingly acquiesced to the host's demand and slowly vacated the room acknowledging his former employees and customers alike with a jaunty, cheeky waving as he slowly departed the function suite.

After an interlude of approximately twenty minutes, Dave Moreland once again returned, this time he was not alone, but instead accompanied by a number of former company Directors and Managers.

Yet again, Dave Pearce approached his predecessor and the other interlopers. However, this time, at the head of this contingent was another Dave, Dave Parry, the former Managing Director, an ex-rugby player about 6 ft 4 inches tall and built like the proverbial brick outhouse. Once again Dave Pearce repeated his monologue, but this time but before he could end it, Dave Parry leaned over to the 5 ft 10 inches of Dave Pearce, grabbed his nose then sadistically, slowly and deliberately began twisting the protuberance on the Area Director's face. The anger welled up in Dave Pearce, who immediately pulled back his right arm to obtain maximum momentum then after, clenching his fist brought it around to connect with Mr. Parry's face, Dave Parry went down, then before long George Morris another miniscule ex-Hyperwaste Manager dived onto Dave Pearce, who because of the force, lost his balance and fell to the floor. Some of the lorry drivers had been given overtime to act as bouncers. They watched in horror at the spectacle unfolding before them, as their former bosses began accosting the new Area Sales Director, not knowing what to do, after all they had been friendly with the ex-managers and directors during their time at the helm and actually had nothing against them, in fact, most of them liked and respected their previous bosses. However, almost immediately,

168

the termination of employment suddenly flashed through their minds, observing their new boss on the floor under a plethora of the former directors. Following a split second of indecision, the drivers decided perhaps they had better help the recently appointed Area Director, who was obviously in difficulty. They did not fancy being unemployed the following week after failing to come to his rescue.

All hell broke loose as ex-Directors, new directors, ex-managers, new managers and drivers became embroiled in a melee on the middle of the prestigious hotel function room. It became complete out–and-out mayhem. The bemused customers just stood and a watched in complete and utter disbelief, totally amazed as bodies writhed on the floor with arms, legs and fists flying in all directions. The sound of the altercation soon came to the attention of the hotel management. Suddenly the number of bodies in the fracas was increased by the not insubstantial frames of the hotel bouncers who joined the affray, desperately trying to put an end to all this unwanted pugilistic activity taking place within the confines of the prestigious hotel.

One of the office girls from one of the South Wales' depots, and who had also consumed quite a bit of alcohol, looked on in utter astonishment at the spectacle taking place in front of her, through her alcoholic, intoxicated haze, as if in some sort of surrealistic dream. Upon looking over to the corner of the room, she observed Ryan Rhys, a person not renowned for his heroism, desperately seeking refuge under one of the larger, more substantial tables, which he evidently considered capable of withstanding the turmoil and pandemonium going on all around him. What surprised the young girl even more, upon further scrutiny of the room was the sight of Dave Moreland, the instigator of all this mayhem, fighting, bedlam and confusion, quite happily sitting in the corner of the room, chatting up three rather attractive, heavily made-up, young ladies, who, shall we say, had been provided as '*company* 'for some of the more important male customers. He appeared to be unconcerned at the mayhem going on in front of him, mayhem which he had provoked. All the while, he flirted outrageously with the young, attractive female escorts.

After a short period of time, the hotel staff and bouncers finally restored order, with everybody, including the innocent bystanders requested firmly but politely to immediately leave the hotel. Hyperwaste were never allowed to use that hotel ever again for entertaining their valued customers. Thanks mainly to Dave Moreland who came out of it all unscathed and knowing Dave with an assignation or two planned for the following week with the '*young ladies*'. You had to admire the guy he had a hell of a lot of cheek, yet an endearing charm and style which he carried off with a certain amount of panache.

International days with Hyperwaste had a certain enjoyment and sense of adventure with a hint of the unknown about them. I later became part of this exciting activity, in which I participated in with unabashed enthusiasm.

Sadly, my father died in 1994. Up until that time, both he and I would always go to one of the local pubs or clubs near to where he then lived with my step-mother to watch the match on a big screen. I had lost not only a father but a very good friend and confidante. I still miss him to this day, the passage of time only slightly diminishing the feeling of loss.

The following Rugby International Season, following my father's death, I began attending the Hyperwaste functions, and with my usual enthusiasm joining in whole-heartedly. Being acquainted with quite

170

a few of the regular customers because of my job also helped. To be quite honest, I am not reserved, especially after ingesting in a few beers. I became friendly with one of the managers from a company called Gwent Galv, called James Clackett. He was a Yorkshire man, originating from Wakefield, but at that time living in Newport. He was your typical, gritty, no-nonsense, straight talking Yorkshire-man. But we got on quite well and became drinking partners, during theses soirees. Being the only technical person at Hyperwaste in the region, I often visited his site on a regularly basis, following some incident or other at the site. We always ended up getting quite merry after ingesting a fair amount of alcoholic beverages. During one match, James walked out into the fresh air from the CIA (Cardiff International Arena), took a deep breath of the cold night air and immediately passed out. Some of the Welsh selectors had to tread carefully over the prostrate body of Mr. Clackett as he lay comatose on the floor, one of them was heard to usher the words,

'Ah, a Mountain Ash boy If ever I saw one!' How the selector ever came to that conclusion is beyond me, for as previously mentioned, James had been born and bred in Wakefield and a proud Yorkshire man. One of his fellow work colleagues picked him up, James hanging onto him like a bedraggled, limp rag doll, unaware of what was happening around him. His friends waited for his wife to collect him in the compact family car.

Upon first observing the scene, his wife thought it was a wind up. Her disbelief turned quickly to anger and annoyance upon discovering her beloved husband was not acting but indeed in an extreme state of intoxication.

The limp body of James was deposited unceremoniously and as quickly as possible on the back seat of the car, his friends being fully aware of his wife's anger and wrath, their main objective became to expedite her departure from the CIA as quickly as possible before being subjected to the vitriolic tirade from her sharp tongue which they had often been subjected to on previous occasions. Once the limp body had been disposed of in the car, his wife belligerently slammed the door shut, then entered the driver's side and departed at high speed, her anger and frustration being vented via the Pirelli tyres of the automobile, evident by the clouds of smoke generated by the screeching tyres as the car hurtled down the busy road. James' friends departed the scene of the crime as quickly as possible in case his other half returned to perform an impulsive 'hit and run' as a form of justified, homicidal retribution on them both.

From what I understand after talking to James sometime later, a considerable period of time elapsed before he and his wife were able to talk civilly to each other following that particular International night out and even more time before carnal relationship was restored.

Another rugby international, following a match in which Wales played Scotland and although putting up, a valiant fight, the home team lost that particular encounter. Once gain James and I thought it only polite to consume as much of the alcohol as possible which had been so generously been provided by my employer. By 6:30 in the evening, all the whisky had been exhausted, and as If that were not enough, we were told to evacuate the room, it having only been booked until 7:00 that evening. Everyone obligingly vacated the room, with an impromptu committee set up to discuss which public house in Cardiff would have the privilege of our company for the remainder of the evening and where we could consume yet more alcohol. With the lucky public house which about to reap the benefits of our presence being undecided, and still in discussion, I made my way to the toilet in order to relieve my highly stressed bladder, where I stumbled upon two Scottish supporters. Rugby is one of those sports where no animosity is held by players or supporters, that is unless it concerns England, but as far as our fellow Celtic teams are concerned it is all good natured. I congratulated the two Scottish supporters on their team winning and got chatting to them, bewailing the fact Wales had lost the match, informing them my colleagues and I had been told to vacate our hospitality room, and the fact is the whisky had been exhausted for some considerable time.

'Och why don't you come into our function room, it's been booked until 8:00 and there's plenty of whisky?' One of them said in a broad Glaswegian accent, meanwhile his friend nodded his head profusely in agreement. Looking from one to the other, peering through an intoxicated haze, it appeared churlish and impolite not to agree to their kind offer, and I had no wish to appear indecorous or aloof and therefore accompanied them to the function room, the three of us staggering along the plush carpet covered corridors of the CIA. Upon entering the function room, one of my new found friends instructed the rather attractive waitress, to pour me a large whisky, addressing her by her first name, obviously having become friendly with her during the day's proceedings. She poured the drink without any argument, exuding an extremely pleasant, attractive and disarming smile. Talking to my new found Scottish friends, it became evident they were only guests and not responsible for the function, which did make me feel slightly uneasy. However the alcohol in my body quickly dispelled any apprehension which I may have felt for that brief second or two. I must admit

173

I had a whale of a time, chatting with complete strangers whom I had never met before and, in all probability would, never meet again.

The hour or so quickly passed until eventually, I was instructed to leave the room, following the entourage of my new found friends down to the street in the cold Cardiff city night air. By now I was thoroughly intoxicated and thought perhaps I had better go in search of my lost colleagues from Hyperwaste. But where the hell did they go? I started working my way through some of the pubs down St Mary's Street, we had previously frequented during other International matches, imbibing in each hostelry we passed. By about 10:30, I asked for a drink in one of the bars, suddenly realizing I could barely talk, so heaven knows how the Barman managed to give me the correct drink, which as I recall was a Jack Daniels and Coke. After slowly consuming the drink, I thought I had better forget about resuming my rather unproductive search for my colleagues from Hyperwaste and head for home, which is what I did, catching a train to Rhymney and as I recall hitch-hiking along the heads of the valley road eventually getting home to a rather irate Stella at about 2 am. in the morning, going to bed and promptly falling asleep.

At other Internationals, such as when Wales played Ireland, I found myself in the crowd at the Arms Park completely surrounded by Irish supporters. However, with it being a rugby match, I felt quite safe and not intimidated at all. Everyone just enjoys the rugby and not out for any trouble which only manifests itself at company functions.

At yet another match, when Wales played against France, the French directors of the company came across the Channel to watch the match and in which Wales beat them, wunderbar. Later that night, I

174

recollect being in one of the pubs, chatting for a considerable period of time to a beautiful chic, French woman named Pascal much to the annoyance of her, angry, jealous husband.

Hyperwaste also helped sponsor Newbridge, one of the local rugby teams. They were playing Llanelli or as they are known to their supporters The Scarlets at Newbridge. Hyperwaste had arranged food in the Newbridge Club House. I was there talking to a couple of the customers including my old friend James Clackett and a couple of the girls who were the 'company' for the higher spending customers. Whilst we all indulged in small talk, in strolled Derek Quinnell, one of the Welsh selectors and iconic player from that wonderful, legendary team of the seventies.

Derek had come to support his son who was playing for the Scarletts. I remember, as most older Welshmen must recall, Derek nearly bowling over a policeman over whilst running through the tunnel over in his efforts to get on to the pitch and win his first Welsh cap before the final whistle blew. Derek's chemical company had supplied materials to my old employer, Repeat Controls and he often bought me lunch a couple of times in an effort to secure the sales of his chemicals. That had been at least eight years earlier and I did not think he would remember me. As he walked into the room, he looked around, saw me and gave a friendly wave. I thought he must have been waving to some other person, not a bit of, it he actually remembered me and came over for a chat. I was non-plussed, to think an esteemed member of the Welsh Squad from the seventies and now a member of the Welsh Selectors, should remembered a lowly process engineer from years gone by. He is a really genuinely friendly nice guy.

My time spent at Hyperwaste and the rugby internationals often invoke fond memories. Alas the company has long since changed, with the tradition of entertaining customers at Rugby International matches no longer thought necessary. I still occasionally go to Internationals, but not as frequently as I once did when employed by Hyperwaste, which is a shame.

CHAPTER 16

*M*ost waste disposal companies at sometime or other, during their existence, invariably become involved with large land reclamation projects. Hyperwaste proved to be no exception, becoming involved with a large reclamation project located in Dowlais, a district Of Merthyr Tydfil, perched on the mountains of South Wales.

In the nineteenth century, Merthyr Tydfil was designated the unofficial capital of Wales, manufacturing the iron for the cannons used in the Battle of Trafalgar, cast in the numerous iron making infernos owned by the ironmaster dynasties of Guest and Crawshay.

During the early days of the reclamation project, I was based at the new depot and mostly ensconced inside my miniscule laboratory, secreted inside the garage workshop. Although on the odd occasions, I tended to package hazardous waste and arrange for authorised disposal in addition to any analysis required. All this interspersed with the sporadic chemical cleaning project for the Middlesborough depot whenever they required the services of a cheap chemist. However, despite all these welcome interludes, life was becoming mundane and certainly not as much fun as my time spent at the treatment plant where Cedric and Jamie obligingly provided the free, comical entertainment, continually bickering like two old maids or Laurel and Hardy.

Dave Pearce had deemed I should become involved with a large reclamation project at Dowlais, a venture in which Hyperwaste looked likely to win the tender as the main hazardous waste contractor. It was intended I should be the resident chemist for the duration of the project, anticipated would last about six to seven weeks. I looked forward to it, for a start it was only 20 minutes from where I now lived with Stella in my old home town.

Gerald Charters my old associate from the West Mercian Oils days now worked as a Sales Representative for Hyperwaste, eventually winning the contract, estimated to be worth at least a quarter of a million pounds and making him the flavour of the month at boardroom level. The main contractor overseeing the project was a civil engineering company called Nanstead.

Regime De L'Aqua, our major company and owner had its fingers in many pies, owning various types of companies encompassing numerous business genres within France, businesses such as Waste Disposal, Civil Engineering, Telecommunications, Medical Care, Railways and God knows what else. All these French companies had, themselves, in turn acquired companies within the UK, UPA had acquired Hyperwaste. Nanstead had been acquired by another company, but ultimately the branches of the tree led to the root which was Regime De L'Aqua with its involvement everywhere. Thus, technically, Hyperwaste and Nanstead came under the auspices of the Regime De L'Aqua empire and could be described as business cousins. There had been a corporate philosophy and directive that wherever possible, everything should be kept 'in house' so Nanstead approached Hyperwaste to handle the waste disposal side for the toxic chemicals on the site and the client was Mid Glamorgan County Council

The story starts about 1992, some contractors were cleaning some drainage pipes located in the vicinity of

178

the Mid-Glamorgan County council offices for the Education Department located in Dowlais. It was during the cleaning operation the contractors noticed a rather large seepage of black viscous tar. Work stopped and investigations carried out and it was discovered there had been a coal gas works located at the site which produced carbon monoxide and coke for the blast furnaces of an old steelworks located there at the end of the nineteenth century up until the mid-twenties of the nineteenth century and now where the new Council offices managed to be located.

Boreholes were dug all around and a multitude of samples taken. To the dismay of the council, its workforce and local residence the whole area was found to be highly contaminated with the by-products of coal gas production, phenol, miscellaneous phenol compounds, polyaromatic hydrocarbons (PAH's), cadmium, mercury, arsenic, coal tars, various oils, cyanide, ammonia. In fact, a whole cocktail of highly toxic, noxious chemical compounds, some of which had proven links with generating cancerous cells in humans. During the days of the coke ovens, less concern had been shown for the environment during the manufacturing and certainly during the closure of the facility.

After the initial investigations, it was decided the whole area would have to be dug up and the contaminated soils removed from the site and safely disposed of. The contamination throughout the site varied in degrees, the amount of contamination would decide where the soil would eventually be disposed of, and there were hazardous waste disposal sites in Wales, which could dispose of the low content waste, less than 2% of oils and PAH's. The highly contaminated soils were to be disposed of in specialised sites in England the initially the site chosen was the Shanks landfill site at Bedford. High Temperature Incineration would have been the best option and most environmentally friendly, but the Council had a limited budget and incineration would prove far too costly, the landfill option deemed to be the most viable final solution. The less contaminated soil ironically would go to an authorized landfill site at Trecatti located a few miles from Dowlais and within the Merthyr catchment area. The initial estimates by the consultants working for the council showed there could be in the region of approximately 6,000 – 8,000 tonnes of contaminated soil to be disposed of. This turned out to be a gross underestimation.

Eventually, Nanstead won the contract becoming the main contracting company supervising the project with Hyperwaste being sub contracted as the waste disposal contractor. There had been a tremendous amount of publicity about the land contamination with all aspects of the media getting involved. The local press, most damaging of all, the local television channel for the principality. BBC Wales, HTV together with S4C, the channel for Welsh speakers.

Because of all this publicity, the local residents became fully aware of what was going on and a general meeting arranged in the local community hall to explain the proposed action being taken to remove and eradicate the toxic contamination. Unfortunately, no one from Hyperwaste wished to attend the meeting and as the proposed resident Chemist for Hyperwaste on the landfill site, I was instructed to put in an appearance which I had no wish to do for two reasons. Firstly, it was at 7 o' clock in the evening and I received no overtime payment and secondly, I hated having to speak to large gatherings, being shy in that respect, particularly with the prospect of facing a potentially hostile audience.

180

Arriving at the meeting hall, I discovered it to be teeming with what can only be described as belligerent, angry residents. The team from Nanstead were there together with local councillors and the executives from Mid-Glamorgan County Council. The councillors called me to one side and began instructing me on what to say to the local action committee.

I was told by the council PR representative, 'The tack to take is that we were there to help the community and not to pollute or damage the environment. If they ask you where the waste is to be taken to, just say "England." Trust me, there will be no need to elaborate anymore.'

I just looked at him incredulously, as both he and I knew the less contaminated soils would actually be disposed of in the landfill site at Trecatti, just a few miles along the 'Heads of the Valley' road and so technically we were being more than frugal with the truth. These councillors were supposed to represent the local community and were in fact lying to the very people they purportedly represented. '*So what's new?*' I hear you saying.

The meeting was quite acrimonious, and I was asked a lot of questions about the transport arrangements. As the 20 tonne tipper trucks would be travelling through the village, it was estimated at the peak to be in the region of 10 - 15 per day. The residents were of course worried about the safety of the local children and possible spillages from the vehicles of the contaminated soil and so a lot of questions related to this issue. These were questions Ryan should have been there to answer, being the transport Manager, but of course it had been left to me. They also asked questions about the types of chemicals contained in the soil. I tried to be as honest as possible, but every time the councillors thought I appeared to be divulging too much information, they would interrupt and cleverly steer the topic of debate away from that particular subject.

Like typical politicians, they appeared quite adept at avoiding any subject they did not wish to discuss. They did, however, point out to the residents present that we were there to help the community and that we were all striving for the same thing, to remove the toxic waste from the ground, in a responsible and environmentally safe manner. Ultimately, after about 90 minutes, the meeting terminated, with the local residents reasonably satisfied with the answers they had received. I arrived home at about 9 o'clock that evening, thoroughly exhausted, it had been a very long day indeed.

The meeting had been held about June 1993, with the intention of commencing work on the removal beginning within a couple of weeks. However, for one reason or another, the work did not begin until, early October of that year. It did however give Hyperwaste much needed time to prepare for the project, I went to the site and took samples of various areas to get an idea of the

Concentrations of the wastes and the content of chemicals, particularly PAH compounds with thousands of pounds were eventually spent on this specialised analysis.

Work finally began in October, slowly at first, with the first soils being removed after a day or so. At first they were lightly contaminated and were disposed of at the local site in Trecatti. Eventually the heavier contaminated soils began to appear and taken to Shanks at Stewart by in Bedfordshire, a huge landfill site, some 160 miles from the contaminated site at Dowlais.

It quickly became evident from the outset that this was going to be totally impracticable, with the vehicles only being capable of making 1½ trip per day, we would need a huge fleet of tipper vehicles to remove the estimated 6,000 tonnes of soil within the six weeks which had been specified in the contract, tipper vehicles at that, a type of vehicle, vehicles which Hyperwaste did not possess in the required large quantities. The main contractor Nanstead requested if we could find a legal suitable landfill site nearer which could take the more heavily contaminated soil called a meeting. As technical advisor I came up with a site at Swindon, some hundred miles down the road. Now the contract had been written in such a way as to leave glaring loopholes. The way in which the contract and description of the waste had been categorised in the contract and costs for the particular category would have dire consequences at the end of the contract, and which I too would become embroiled. The lightly contaminated solids could be disposed of within 100 miles of the site at Dowlais. The highly contaminated soils would be disposed of over 100 miles the cost for disposal for the low contamination would be low at somewhere in the region of £16 per tonne with £3 per tonne transport. Originally the heavier contaminated soil would have to be disposed of at Stewart by some 160 miles, well over the 100 miles for highly contaminated soil at £30 per tonne plus £5 per tonne transport. Hills, the waste contactor at Swindon sent some representatives to the Dowlais site to evaluate the waste. I had had contact with the personnel and knew them well. This made things easier. Ryan was asked the question by Gerald Charters before the meeting, a question which he asked, in my presence.

'Ryan it is over 100 miles from Merthyr to Hills at Swindon?' Ryan answered in his usual nonchalant, flippant way.

'No problem well over yes…. don't worry.' Gerald appeared to be reasonably satisfied with Ryan's

183

answer, although I suspect he did not know at that time the meeting with Hills went very well. The representatives from Hills were happy they were able to dispose of the waste legally at their site. They took some samples to be on the safe side. The price for disposal was acceptable to them and to Hyperwaste, everything was looking good. The customer, Mid-Glamorgan County Council had no problem with the disposal site as long as the waste was removed of safely, and efficiently, with the proviso in the budget that removal of the 5,000 - 6000 tonnes of soil would not be affected.

The job got under way in earnest the waste being sent to Hills with the vehicles making 2 ½ trips per day, almost doubling the removal rate using one 20 tonne tipper vehicle when using the Stewartby site in Bedford. I was on site with my old mate Karl Barclay, two other labourers from Hyperwaste. Karl supervised the loading and sheeting of the waste and I, together with the consultant chemist working for the council, decided whether the waste was lightly or heavily contaminated the lightly contaminated soil to Trecatti, the highly contaminated soils to Swindon. I was enjoying the job working at the coal face, and hands on, metaphorically speaking. Although the weather began to become cold wet and miserable, I was thoroughly enjoying it.

Gradually giant holes began appearing around the site as if a giant rodent had been frantically burrowing on the site. The giant holes generated caused another problem, some of the holes still had contamination in them and when the rains came, began to fill up with the precipitation, which itself became contaminated with the coal tars. For this reason the work on the site should have started in the summer during the dry weather. However because of the late time of year this caused the water contamination problem. The contaminated water had to be taken to water treatment sites for disposal because of these coal tars. This generated extra costs which had not been budgeted for by the council, also as the digging progressed, it became evident considerably more than 5,000 tonnes of soil were going to have to be removed to eliminate all the contamination to the site and probably more in the region of 15,000 - 20,000 tonnes. It was up to the consultancy firm advising the council to determine when the areas had been sufficiently cleared not Hyperwaste. They told us to keep digging and discussions between the consultant chemist and me deciding where the waste was to be disposed of. The holes were getting deeper and the rains came down with a vengeance, necessitating tankers frequently being required to remove the contaminated water, and the costs escalated exponentially. Samples were taken by the consultancy company for analysis to determine if areas could be safely backfilled, analysis which took over a week before completion. I did a bit of PR work, and saved the customer some money, after contacting Welsh Water to discuss the removal of the rain water in holes, which I considered to have little if any at all contamination, asking them if we could pump the water straight into the foul sewers. Again, it was a contact I had dealings with previously. We discussed the volumes to be removed, his main concern being whether the drains could take the extra volume being discharged, with the high amount of rainfall being experienced, higher than normal in fact. Eventually, we agreed in discharge rates and costs for disposal, which were far less than costs of taking the water out by 20 tonne tanker. Mid-Glamorgan County Council was ecstatic with the outcome, not so Ryan Rhys who lost extra revenue for his tanker fleet.

185

Accompanying the rains, we also experienced high winds, which made it impossible to put the tarpaulin on the vehicles to cove the hazardous materials. The general location of the project did not help, the site being perched on top of a mountain exposed to the vagaries of the climactic elements. Karl and I considered it unsafe for the team to try and sheet the vehicles with heavy gale force winds and so this also held up the removal of the soil.

We utilised drivers from other Hyperwaste depots helping us out, two of which came from one of the northern depots, one of which was a guy called Stuart, who turned out to be quite a ladies' man, despite being married. He managed to strike up a '*friendship*' with a lady from Purton, the local village nearest to the disposal site. Stuart had become very 'friendly' with this lady, which resulted in him sleeping at her house during his time in Purton. I remember him phoning me one windy day to ask if it was worth travelling from Purton to Dowlais that day because of the high winds buffeting the country, as he would be unable to have his vehicle loaded and sheeted so he may as well leave early the next day from Purton. He would phone me later that morning to

We were being pressurised by Nanstead because of the lost time and so it was imperative to lose as little time as possible. I phoned Cardiff Wales airport to get an update on the weather conditions. They informed me, there was a high probability the winds would abate by mid-afternoon. I told Stuart to drive back to Dowlais and that his vehicle would be loaded that afternoon and he could return to Purton the same evening.

Stuart arrived with his vehicle about 3:30 pm the afternoon only to discover the winds had unfortunately not abated as predicted and he could not be loaded until the next morning and would have to spend the night in

Merthyr Tydfil, not embraced in the warm inviting arms and ample bosoms of his new lady friend in her cosy double bed.

He was not a happy bunny and kept bemoaning the fact he was stuck in Merthyr Tydfil for the night. I told him we were there to do a job and not for the benefit of his sex life, even though he disagreed considering it to be his main priority. In all fairness he took the situation stoically. Thankfully, next day, the winds abated, with Stuart able to spend the next night cuddled up alongside the warm body of his female lover in her substantial, comfortable warm bed.

The love, or rather lust affair ended shortly afterwards with the somewhat unexpected and unwanted return of her psychopathic, paranoid, violent husband who was out on probation from his place of incarceration where he had been serving a sentence after inflicting grievous bodily harm on some poor unfortunate individual. This unexpected return of the lady's husband necessitated Stuart having to make a somewhat frantic exit from his lover's boudoir and running naked down the dark streets in the early hours of the morning, desperately clutching his clothing which flapped about like a wind sock in a high wind in the slip stream behind him, hoping his descent down the rusty, fragile drainpipe had not been observed by his lover's anti-social, psychopathic husband. After his escape Stuart did not have any visible form of injuries after that fateful night, so I guess he must have been successful in getting away without the husband observing him.

Some of the other drivers also became involved with females while driving on the reclamation project also availing them of the chance to sleep in the comfort of welcoming beds alongside a sexually active female.

Occasionally, the ability to charm the fairer sex females generated some friction between some of the drivers.

Tommy Morgan had been trying to become friendly with a female who often accompanied Stuart's lover to the local pub in Purton. For a few weeks he had been chatting to her in the local pub which the two women often frequented. Tommy desperately attempted turning on the charm. Having been divorced for over a year, one could say Tommy was greatly in need of female company to relieve the sexual tension which had been accumulating inside him during all that time. Unfortunately for Tommy, he did not have a lot going for him, suffering from disgusting body odour, he was grossly obese and overweight carrying a huge beer pot and not particularly good looking with some vile, disgusting habits. An example of his disgusting habits was brought home to me while based at the new depot. Phil, one of the diesel fitters, was cleaning what he erroneously believed to be dried resin from a local paint factory off the driver's side window of Tommy's vehicle which had been in for plating or MOT as known for cars. Tommy often took his vehicle into the paint factory for waste collection so this could not be considered unreasonable. While Phil desperately tried to extricate the resin from the glass, one of the other fitters came up to him and enquired.

'What do you think you are removing from the window, Phil?'

'Paint resin,' Phil replied, naively.

Jacob the other fitter then replied whilst exuding a somewhat broad sadistic, smile on his face.

'That's what you think, that's Tommy Morgan's cab and you know what he has a habit of doing, spitting out of his cab, which often goes straight onto the window?' Phil suddenly stopped rubbing the window of the cab with his, now heavily '*resin*' impregnated cloth. An

188

incongruent facial mixture of disgust, revulsion and horror appeared on his rotund features, while indulging in these facial contortions, throwing down the resin impregnated cloth as fast as he could, as if it had just spontaneously combusted in his hand. He then ran into the nearby toilets before indulging in projectile vomiting.

Tommy's manners, and habits were uncouth and his general bad attitude left a lot to be desired. The woman in question told him she had recently split up with her boyfriend, whom allegedly had been long-standing relationship and all she wanted was a platonic relationship with no intention, for the present, in becoming romantically involved with another man. However, her attitude amended quite considerably when Jack Jones appeared on the scene. Jack was another driver from the same depot. He and Tommy were good friends. Jack was totally different to Tommy. He was slim, reasonably good looking, suave, well-dressed, particularly when out socialising. He also possessed a wicked sense of humour, good manners and the innate ability to charm the pants off women, which is precisely what he did with Tommy's lady friend. Within a few days of travelling down to Swindon, after being seconded on to the project, Jack ended up in the boudoir of the very woman Tommy had been desperately attempting to seduce and without any hint of success, for weeks. It had been an uneven contest in winning the lady's favour from the outset, with poor Tony standing no chance whatsoever. Needless to say, the former friendship between Tommy and Jack ended then and there. From that time onwards, the two drivers made certain they were never in Swindon at the same time. Fortunately, Jack left Hyperwaste shortly afterwards to work for another waste transport company.

189

CHAPTER 17

*T*he days on the landfill site turned into weeks, which themselves turned into months. October became November then December. The weather turned cold and most decidedly inclement. Some days even resulting in the site being covered in a thick blanket of crisp, virgin snow, because of the location, being elevated so high up in the Welsh Valleys, the snow hung around for a considerable period of time. It soon become evident the estimated 6,000 tonnes of contaminated soil to be removed would be greatly exceeded, and the County Council began getting extremely concerned about the escalating costs. It was apparent they were going to exceed the budgeted amount and not by an insubstantial amount either. It was then one of the on-site managers for the County Council, a young boy whom Karl Barclay nicknamed The Muppet, but whose name happened to be Horace asked an unfortunate question. There was a mutual antipathy between Karl and Horace which both did not conceal from the other. The latter hoped to gain some brownie points by trying to cut the amount which would have to be paid to contractors, primarily Hyperwaste.

The dreaded question which the Muppet asked was, 'Is it 100 miles from Dowlais to the landfill site at Swindon?' From then onwards, Ryan Rhys became obliged to supply the odometer readings on each vehicle making the trip to verify the distance did exceed the 100 miles for the highly contaminated soil. The readings indicated on the vehicles odometers indicated the distance to be in the region of 101.2 miles from the weigh bridge at Dowlais to the weighbridge at the, landfill site on the outskirts of Swindon Wiltshire, only slightly exceeding the specified 100 miles mentioned in the contract but still in Hyperwaste's favour and adhering to the terms of the contract.

The County Council however, were not satisfied with these reading, insisting upon Hyperwaste hiring a properly calibrated car for the journey, with a special wheel at the back with the ability to measure distances to the nearest half metre, adding salt to the wound, with the vehicle to be hired at Hyperwaste's expense. Documentation had to be provided by the company beforehand showing they had measured racing circuits throughout the world and had carried out measurements for the Ford Motor Corporation, Formula 1, BMW, Mercedes and General Motors to mention a few, quite an impressive portfolio in fact.

The day arrived for the vehicle to carry out the measurement of the distance between Dowlais and Purton. There were number of anxious and nervous people about, particularly Gerald, who had been instructed to accompany the Muppet following the special vehicle, travelling his company car. After all, it was he who had set up the contract with the generalised statement stipulating he magic threshold of 100 miles, and now the prospect of Hyperwaste standing to lose small fortune seemed possible.

The reader can do the maths. It was costing £30 per tonne disposal at Purton for the highly contaminated soil, plus the cost of fuel and driver's wages. It was only costing in the region of £12 per tonne for disposal of the lightly contaminated soil at the local site at Trecatti with much less fuel costs. If the overall cost for disposal had to be revised down to £20 from £40 per tonne across the board, then Hyperwaste would lose probably well in excess of £150,000. The amount of

191

soil removed at that time approached the region of 10,000 tonnes with large areas of the site still to be investigated. It looked as if the amount to be removed would be in the region of 25,000 - 30,000 tonnes and nowhere near the figure originally forecast by the environmental consultants employed by the council.

So if the contract was to be suddenly turned on its head, Hyperwaste could lose a fortune. By December, that particular figure appeared to be approaching £180,000. But if the amount of soil removed approached 25,000 tonnes, which seemed likely, that figure would be approaching a £400,000 loss to Hyperwaste and by the time everything was considered, the amount could be approaching half a million pounds and maybe more. The County Council were losing money as they had budgeted for the removal of only 6,000 tonnes and were at 10,000 tonnes and still rising. The whole venture was proving to be disastrous for all concerned. One heavy plant hire company supplying diggers and Euclid's went bankrupt because they had not put enough penalty clauses into their contract for delays to the project due to bad weather and awaiting analysis results for areas which had been excavated. They finally went bankrupt and unable to pay their drivers. One driver Jason even broke into his employer's offices and stole some laptops as recompense for his work for which he had not been paid. The police quickly arrested him. The last I heard, his case was pending in a few months.

After the measurement exercise, the figures came back from the company with the calibrated measuring vehicle, the distance between the weigh bridges at Dowlas to the weigh bridge at Purton using a Mondeo, indicated a distance of 99.2 miles, not 101.2 as indicated on the 20 tonne articulated tippers' odometers.

Gerald became extremely concerned about his job and position within the company, with Hyperwaste now on the point of losing a fortune, due to the contract, a contract which he had set up on his own. Ryan Rhys however continued to ask the driver's for their odometer readings which consistently indicated the mileage to be 101.2 miles from weighbridge to weigh bridge. Why the difference between the car and the tippers? After investigating and research, it became evident articulated vehicles because of their length, to negotiate safely had to swing wide around roundabouts and corners, the extra few metres travelled each time, added up to give an overall distance of 101.2 miles.

Arguments became heated. Unfortunately, Nanstaed sided with the Council in stating they thought the distance should be taken as 99.2 miles, and not the higher reading. The dispute became quite acrimonious, Tom Driscoll the Hyperwaste MD phoned the MD for Nanstead to discuss the situation, which itself ended up with them both uttering profanities and bellowing at each other down the telephone line and must have been one hell of a telephone conversation.

Barristers and solicitors were hired by Hyperwaste and the County Council to try and ascertain which constituted the true mileage in the terms of the contract, by car or articulated vehicle, with both sides standing to lose a great deal both legal parties argued their case vociferously on behalf of their respective clients.

By this time at the beginning of the year in February, I had to take some time off work. I had developed a double hernia, and the doctors considered it prudent for me to have an operation to cure the problem as soon as possible. So in February I had to go into Neville Hall, an NHS Hospital in Abergavenny for the operation, not before Paul, the Quantity surveyor working for Nanstead took great pleasure in supplying me with the statistics concerning the amount of people dying in an operation due to an overdose of anaesthetic. When he could see I could not be wound up concerning his statement he gave up. Personally, I cannot think of a better way of dying, under a massive amount of anaesthetic, peacefully and with no pain.

Roger was a character. He is the only Rugby linesman I know who has been sent off the pitch by the referee for fighting with a rugby player during a match after he hurtled onto the pitch during a local derby and beat the shit out of a forward who was giving the scrum half for his team a rough time.

For anyone who has little experienced a hernia operation, it means at least six weeks lay up without physical exertion and heavy movement, certainly no driving. This meant I had to be taken off the land reclamation project for the last few weeks of its duration. It had been anticipated by that time the project would have been completed and so the operation would have not been a problem, however it was still on-going because of the amount of contamination still being unearthed so Gerald had to take over the site chemist's duties until completion. I meanwhile worked from home, answering questions from the depots and supplying them with Technical Advice documents for shipping waste, which I had been doing from the portacabin on the landfill site. Hyperwaste had supplied me with a computer, printer, modem, fax machine and mobile telephone to go with the landline and so I could remain in contact with everyone from home. But returning to the landfill site was impossible due to the time required for rest and recuperation.

At that time, my relationship with Stella started on the slippery, downward slope resulting in us eventually calling it a day a few years down the line. On my first night home from hospital, she had gone out with some of her female friends. Not an issue as far as I was concerned, that is until she returned home late that same evening extremely intoxicated and incapable of doing anything for herself. Before she left the house for her evening's enjoyment, I had almost pleaded with her, requesting her not to drink too much. When she returned home, Stella was so drunk, I had to get her a plastic bowl in which she could vomit and regurgitate her evening's meal over the bed clothes. Remember I had just returned from hospital following a double hernia operation and the doctors told I should not even make myself a cup of tea. From that night onwards, I lost all feelings for the woman I had once loved passionately, she killed the magic. The next week she added fuel to the fires of mounting animosity by taking the painkillers that the surgeons had given me to alleviate the pain of the operation. I was in absolute agony and whilst looking for the tablets, Stella casually informed me 'I've been taking them for my headache, I took the last one this morning.'

As casually if it had been my last Rollo in the pack, she had eaten the tablets which would alleviate the excruciating pain I tended to be experiencing following my operation. She obviously had no consideration for me at all. Cindy, my ex-wife would never have done such a thing. It was not long before Stella and I split up after following a few more disastrous incidents due to her sometimes excessive drinking which altered her personality for the worse. I have also had a few nights when I became intoxicated and sound more than hypocritical, but I always fell in love with the world after a few drinks. Stella on the other hand always ended up wanting to fight the world and more often than not, experiencing a metamorphosis into a nasty, belligerent individual after consuming alcohol.

195

The land reclamation project eventually came to a close with no need for me to return to the site. I believed that was the end of the saga. How wrong could I have been? Returning to work, I discovered the disagreement about whether it was over or less than 100 miles between Dowlais and Purton still continued to be a canker, and festering sore between Hyperwaste, Nanstead and the County Council, the three main protagonists. With allegedly the arguments between Tom Driscoll and his counterpart at Nanstead becoming acrimonious to such an extent that both their superiors in France became involved, trying to calm the now bitter dispute between the two of them. After all antipathy between two MD's working for the same multinational company did not look good with this dispute escalating because of a third party, namely the County Council.

The formal litigation between the parties began taking effect with, once again, the barristers on all sides rubbing their avaricious, grasping hands with glee at the prospect of making more money out of this corporate dispute.

Upon my return to work after my enforced convalescence, I was instructed together with Ryan Rhys and Gerald Charters to attend a meeting with the company solicitor at the Hyperwaste Head Office in Manchester to discuss the case concerning the on-going saga. All three of us travelled to the Head Office in Ryan's company car with both he and Gerald arguing about the distance between Dowlais and Purton and Gerald informing Ryan in no uncertain terms he had been misled when told that the distance between the two sites was well over 100 miles and would not be an issue. We had to travel from South Wales to Manchester to be interrogated by a lawyer about the issue which Ryan said from the outset would not be a problem.

Getting to the head office, we were informed by Dave Pearce that I was to be the first victim. And so after a quick cup of coffee, I entered the lion's den. But as I entered thought, *'Why am I worrying so much? It's our solicitor, he will be on our side he will be there to help and advice about the case?'* I was wrong once again on a couple of points. Firstly, he turned out to be a female, and a very attractive one at that. I estimated her to be in her early thirties. Secondly, despite being attractive, as far as the law was concerned, she was a barracuda. The discussion began with her asking me to explain my part in the project. When I began by explaining the route for disposal of the waste, she became quite aggressive.

'And who decided where the waste soil was to go for disposal?'

'Well,' I answered thoughtfully, 'the decision mostly tended to be agreed after a discussion between myself and Steve, The Consultant Environmental Chemist for Mid-Glamorganshire County Council.'

Before I could go any further she interjected, 'That is not what he said, stating the disposal site was always your decision and your decision alone. It was always your decision and he had no say in the matter.'

I replied angrily 'That is not the truth, we always discussed it admittedly not 100% of the time due to him not being available all the time but certainly 80 per cent and whenever he was on site, he had an input as to the final destination of the waste.'

She continued, 'He says he had no input whatsoever the decisions were always yours when you were the site chemist for Hyperwaste.

I was not pleased being questioned about my integrity. 'That is not how I saw it, he always had an input.' This line of cross questioning, continued for a while until she was convinced I was consistent and telling the truth as far as I was concerned.

'Okay,' she continued, 'we'll move onto why the waste went to the different sites. What were the criteria?'

'Mostly visual,' I explained. 'If the soil looked heavily contaminated with tars then they tended to go to Purton.'

'What do you mean by contaminated, qualify and quantify that statement?' she persisted

'Did you have any chemical analysis to that effect for each load?' she badgered.

'No, it's impossible. Every truck load would have to be completely mixed to homogenise the contents and then a few representative samples taken from each load and sent away for analysis which in itself could take three days or more. It would mean five vehicles per day ending up waiting for the whole procedure with a backlog of 15 to 20 vehicles, completely impracticable.'

'You mean to tell me,' she persisted, 'that all the waste sent to Purton was based on purely a visual assessment so all the waste which went to Purton at the higher priced rate was on your word and your word alone?'

'No, as I said before, it was not entirely on my say so, but yes, it was on a visual assessment, backed by experience and background information,' I replied, adding, 'Whose side are you on anyway, I thought you were our solicitor?" With that, her stony, hard-faced lawyer's expression relented slightly and I thought I perceived the hint of a tiny smile.

'I am,' she replied, 'I'm just giving you a taste of what it will be like if it goes to court and you have to take the stand. Believe me if it does go to court my interrogation is as nothing compared to the grilling you will get from their Barrister. They will try to prove you sent a lot of the waste to Purton purely for monetary gain and not based on any technical or chemical reasons.'

'If it was for purely monetary gain for Hyperwaste, I would not have helped the council with the cheaper disposal for the contaminated rain water down the sewer instead of using Hyperwaste Tankers.'

'Good point,' she said, whilst at the same time adding some more scribbles to the copious notes she had been making during our discussion. Our talk continued for about an hour, with Lucrezia Borgia, our solicitor, continually cross-questioning me. I began experiencing self-doubt concerning my part in the project. Finally, she ended the discussion telling me it would be necessary for me to see her again if the case ever went to court.

I left that meeting feeling as if I were responsible for all the evil in the world and also feeling as if all this litigation was entirely my fault. I dreaded the prospect of the case going to court where, under intense cross questioning by the council's determined and aggressive barrister, I would probably end up confessing to being Jack the Ripper or being the perpetrator some other unsolved historical crime.

My ordeal was as nothing compared with the purgatory which Gerald and Ryan had to endure. I had spent just over an hour with Lucrezia Borgia, whereas, Barry spent almost two hours with her and Ryan Rhys a marathon three. Both looked ashen faced and haggard when they finally emerged from the room which had strangely doubled as a court room and mental torture chamber.

Fortunately, the dispute never went to court and none of us subjected to intensive aggressive questioning by some stony-faced Barrister for the opposition. I believe all parties came to a compromise which resulted in Hyperwaste just about 'breaking even' financially. Thankfully, all other costs such as my time and the other people on site came under a separate part of the contract and not included as part of the disposal costs.

It had been quite an eye opener for me as far as Civil Engineering projects are concerned, with the wording of the contract going into minute detail.

Gerald became an outcast and pariah as far as Dave Pearce and the company were concerned, no longer flavour of the month and not authorized to write any more contracts for large projects, with instructions any high value special contracts to be sorted out by Dave Pearce or one of the other managers.

The project dragged on weeks after it should have been completed, due to previous vacillation on the Council's part. During my time on site and just before Christmas, one of the brick cylindrical underground tanks, which had been excavated, appeared to have tar leaching from the outside and through the brickwork with the edge of the brick tank supporting one side of the Council Office Buildings. The tars leaching through looked as if they were coming from underneath the foundations of the Council building itself.

After perusing through old drawings of the site, it became evident the building had been sited above some old tar storage tanks. Someone in the planning department had dropped a momentous bollock. The buildings had been erected in the late sixties, less than 30 years old. No doubt the person responsible still worked for the council and was by now probably very high up the management tree. To clear the old storage tanks could only be done after the council building had been demolished, there was no other way to access

200

them. The council vacillated about what to do. By this time, I had moved onto other projects such as setting up a new treatment plant in Newport.

In 2001, I drove to the site for my own edification. The original council building still stood on the site and appeared to be exactly the same. So obviously the tanks must probably still be intact under the building and still underneath the foundations with the tars still inside them.

Despite all that work had been carried out and I surmise there is still toxic material lying under the building. So I believe the council never did completely eradicate all the toxic waste from the old coke ovens site as promised in order to camouflage their ineptitude.

Overall, it had been yet another very interesting experience in the world of toxic waste.

CHAPTER 18

*P*edantic workaholics exist in all companies and other miscellaneous, diverse walks of life, doing everything by the book. Colours do not exist in their world, only appearing as black and white, with no room for other shades to distort or cause confusion with their assessment of any given situation. Using the modern day, popular vernacular they are often referred to as '*jobsworth*.' In the case of Hyperwaste, the '*jobsworth*' existed in the form of Angela Tate.

By the time I began working for the company in 1989, Angela held the position of Office Manager based at the new business Headquarters located on the outskirts of Manchester. She had first worked for a small company located in the Welsh steel town of Port Talbot. Her employer later became assimilated into the rapidly expanding Hyperwaste Empire. It was while working at this former independent company she and one of the managers, Roger Tate embarked upon a passionate affair. During their relationship, Roger was married to an ex-beauty queen. No-one could comprehend why Roger started the affair, for Angela was certainly no oil painting and putting it bluntly, quite plain looking, with no alluring feminine figure to speak of. Whilst, from all accounts, Roger's wife was quite a stunner with a fantastic, hour glass figure, which is precisely what one would expect with her having the title, ex-beauty queen. Still there may have been unknown circumstances, of which, no-one else had any idea as to why Roger and Angela became lovers. Angela may have possessed hidden attributes, especially in the bedroom department, of which only she and Roger were blissfully aware. They were even rumoured to having been caught indulging in extra marital, horizontal activity on the large expensive mahogany table in the Port Talbot Depot's conference room. One can only hope they did no lasting damage to the varnish and surface of the expensive table.

The inevitable transpired once the affair became knowledge, Roger and his ex-beauty queen wife divorced she citing him for adultery with Angela. Shortly after the Decree Absolute came through, Roger and Angela hastily married in secret. Angela was not pregnant so it was indeed love.

When the original company, for which Roger and Angela worked, became part of the ever expanding Hyperwaste Empire, Roger slowly climbed the company ladder, eventually being elevated to a position on the board of Directors. He and Angela relocated to Manchester with his new wife given the position of Office Manager. All this occurred about the time I joined the company. I began having contact with the personnel at Head Office and it was through these dealings with the office staff, discovered how much of a martinet Mrs. Tate actually was, ruling the office with an iron fist, berating and humiliating people in the open plan office, often in front of their peers, most definitely not the correct way to manage people, causing discontent within the staff who worked under her. First rule of management is, always give bollockings in private and out of earshot of other personnel, not create a spectacle in front of the whole room. I remember that from my altercation with Dean Crabbe in the seventies, all those years earlier, while working at Birchwater and when I was on the receiving end. Too many official complaints soon generated against Angela to be ignored and it eventually became necessary to remove her from her position as Office Manager. Had she not been

Roger's wife, in all probability her career with the company would have ended then and there with her dismissal, however because of her director husband, she continued to be employed by the company in other capacities.

Downsizing, techno-speak for sackings and redundancy, was being instigated within Hyperwaste, as Tom Driscoll began imposing his authority. Gradually the original Directors and friends of Samuel Abbott and Dave Parry found themselves unemployed. Roger Tate was not one of their clique and a survivor somehow managing to keep his position and status within the company.

My friend and colleague ex-sea captain Fred Germaine became part of the casualties because of his close personal friendship with Dave Parry. This meant there was now an opening for a Health and Safety Manager and someone to instigate BS 5740 or ISO 9001 Quality system being imposed upon industry. After the obligatory six months of making a position within the company redundant, Roger nominated Angela to fill this vacant position. Tom Driscoll readily agreed. It also seemed the ideal solution in getting Angela out of the Manchester office, with her causing so much discontent, generating a high turnover of valuable personnel at the headquarters, yet without resorting to sacking her.

Roger's wife took to her new position like a duck to water, after firstly embarking upon expensive Health and Safety and the new ISO 9001quality system training courses. Unfortunately, her new position did absolutely nothing to improve her personnel management skills. Everyone dreaded a quality audit by the 'witch' as she was known. Angela was in her late thirties had apparently, given one of the traffic controllers Neil Peters based in Cheshire a berating and dressing down in front of the whole office for not having the proper systems and paperwork in place. Neil apparently was visibly shaken by this experience. Being in his early sixties, a great grandfather and near retirement, he was unaccustomed to being patronized in such a way, especially in front of the people who worked under him and by someone half his age. Shortly afterwards and following the death of his wife from cancer, poor Neil left the company, opting for early retirement. As he told me over the phone, during his last week with the company, he had enough money put aside for his retirement and did not have to tolerate such hassle and abuse at his time of life.

Unfortunately, Angela also transferred these attitudes into her private life. Whenever she and Roger dined at a restaurant, her first action was automatically to determine the locations of the Fire extinguishers in that particular establishment, inspecting them thoroughly, checking whether they complied with the assessment period and checked within the previous twelve months. Woe-betide any premises which had not had their fire extinguishers inspected within the specified period. Angela would calmly ask to speak to the manager or owner. When the person in charge made an appearance, she would inform them of their misdemeanour and non-compliance, before adding she would return within the month and if the fire extinguishers had not been fully checked out by the manufacturer, would tell the relevant authorities, that is to say the Fire Brigade, who would then possibly prosecute them. Having put the fear of God into the restaurateur, Angela and Roger would then order their meal, no doubt at a reduced rate as a form of inducement not to take matters further. Also true to her word, she and Roger would return to the premises within a few weeks.

What amazed me was the fact Angela was unashamed or embarrassed concerning her behaviour, even informing some of the company staff of her actions with more than a hint of pride. Angela also inspected any hotels in which she stayed, avidly seeking out escape exits, ensuring they were not blocked or obstructed and of course the obligatory fire extinguishers.

If a hotel was remiss in any of its duties, once again Angela read the riot act to the person in charge. The owners of hotels and restaurants must have loved seeing Angela and Roger coming into their premises for a meal and then inspecting the premises as soon as they entered the door, like some hotel or environmental health inspector

Having made this comment about Angela, she was not the only person with this 'foible' and eccentricity the External Quality Auditor being exactly the same, admitting to me he too avidly weighed products at home with his state of the art weighing scales, often writing letters to the manufacturers if he found any shortfalls in their products. It must be the mentality of people involved in quality systems with the ethos having become ingrained in their psyche.

Angela did not generate an imposing figure, being short at five feet three inches, slightly built with a slightly endearing Scottish accent, which was the only endearing thing about her. Angela put the fear of God into more people at Hyperwaste than anyone else I can recall. She did, however, absolutely adore and worship Roger and vice versa. He obviously treasured her, which is why he tolerated her idiosyncrasies.

Angela was undoubtedly one of those people out there on her own, a proud standard bearer for the dedicated *jobs worth*.

CHAPTER 19

*D*uring the treatment plant's final year of existence, both Richard Cooper and Dave Pearce became involved with a large chemical company, which had taken the executive decision to completely close one of its manufacturing facilities located on the outskirts of Swansea.

The ancient, obsolete chemical plant contained miscellaneous hazardous, toxic chemicals which the company had to remove prior to vacating the site in compliance with the environmental laws. The main point of contact within Techno-Chem, the company in question, was the Plant Manager, Steve Houghton. Both Richard and Dave had extensive dealings with Steve, who, we shortly discovered, could be an annoying pedant stickler for minute details, with high expectations and demands. His requirements, included constant attention from the Hyperwaste sales and management team. When women are constantly seeking attention from their partners, they are referred to as being '*high maintenance*' and the Techno-Chem manager most definitely fell into the category of a high maintenance customer.

Following months of protracted negotiations, Hyperwaste and Techno-Chem finally agreed upon an initial contract for disposal of all surplus chemicals at the, now defunct, Swansea facility, with Hyperwaste sourcing then arranging transportation and disposal of all the chemicals. Dave Pearce delegated Richard Cooper the task of project managing the job with assistance and guidance from him whenever required.

Poor Richard, as if he did not have enough on his plate, firstly running a treatment plant, continually embroiled in running battles with demonstrators, together with the local council and finally being elevated to Manager for the whole of the UK Hyperwaste waste division necessitating driving the length and breadth of the country, he now had this major project thrown at him, having to cope with a difficult, meddlesome, obdurate customer.

As initially feared, Steve Houghton proved to be no easy customer to accommodate. In fact, he proved to be even worse than anticipated, demanding a prohibitively, excessive amount of time be allocated to him. Managers and directors for other customers only required removal and disposal of waste in a proper, legal manner, happy to put the onus onto the hazardous waste contractor, contenting themselves with remaining in the background and not becoming involved with the minutiae of the detail. Not so in the case of Steve Houghton, he wanted to keep his waste separate from other materials being disposed of at designated treatment facilities.

This was no easy feat. With compatible acids from different waste producers, upon arrival at the treatment facility, generally mixed together in huge tanks or vats. When sufficient quantity of treatable material accumulated in the vessel, the agglomerated concoction was then treated as a batch. Steve wanted all his waste to be treated separately and the generated neutralised hydroxide sludge kept apart from other inert materials, before finally putting his company's hydroxide solid into its own specially segregated '*cell,*' fundamentally its own grave or plot in the ground at the designated landfill site. For most waste disposal facilities, these special requirements were out of the question, beyond the pale, totally impracticable and not worth the hassle.

208

Richard approached numerous disposal facilities but after going over the stringent treatment requirements, one by one, gradually each declined the business.

Steve continually demanded a prohibitive amount of personal attention, like a spoiled child, forever on the phone to Richard Cooper demanding updates and *'feedback'* on latest developments, insisting he be *'kept in the loop.'* The project began impinging markedly upon Richard's valuable time. After much searching, Richard managed in locating some waste companies willing to put up with these stringent demands required of them. However, that was not the end of it. Steve Houghton insisted upon visiting the intended treatment and landfill sites, which, on some occasions he rejected for various reasons known only to himself.

For Richard Cooper, this meant going back to the drawing board and searching for yet more waste disposal outlets. Often, when he ran out of ideas, Richard would ask me for any possible treatment plants which I knew of throughout the UK. After weeks of this he was on the verge of pulling out what little hair he had left on his head. Of course, all these extra demands and requirements upon disposing of the waste came at a financial price, and Richard ended up having discussions with the outlets and then approaching his difficult client about additional costs for the extra service. Yet again, putting more demands upon his precious time.

Finally, Steve Houghton eventually agreed to use a disposal site, much to Richard's relief. The project concerning Techno-Chem finally came to it end, just about the time we received the news the facility would be closing completely, necessitating 'all hands to the pump,' including Richard, in ensuring the closure and dismantling of the plant was completed on or before the end of January 1992, the stipulated deadline.

Regrettably, that was not the last we heard of the pedantic Steve Houghton. Throughout the life of the project as well as persistently haranguing Richard, he had been ingratiating himself with Dave Pearce. I suspect because Steve knew he would no longer have a job following the closure of the Swansea facility, he wormed his way into obtaining a position within Hyperwaste after giving the company the contract in removing the chemicals from his site. Of course, it worked both ways. Dave Pearce also kept him sweet so as not to lose the lucrative contract, even though it was proving to be more troublesome than first thought.

Following the closure of the Treatment plant, Richard moved down to Cardiff before moving into the new facility. Unfortunately he had upset one of the depot managers who put in a complaint about him to Dave Pearce and a close friend after their time together working for another company. The upshot was the depot manager did not like having a dressing down from Richard who had criticised him in no uncertain terms about not pulling his weight and not generating enough business for the depot in Hertfordshire, just sitting in the office all day drinking coffee. Unfortunately for Richard, the manager was also one of Peter Neil's cohorts as well as being friendly with Dave Pearce, mainly because of their previous association with their former employer.

Both The Managing Director and Dave Pearce sided with Dick Protheroe the depot manager in question. Gradually as the months progressed, Richard began to be more and more side-lined and given difficult duties and treated like a pariah by the Directors, until eventually he was given the unenviable, virtually impossible task of resurrecting the industrial cleaning depot at Port Talbot and where the original headquarters for the company had been situated during its inaugural days. The Port Talbot depot had lost a lot of key personnel who, after leaving purloined quite substantial contracts in the nearby giant steelworks upon joining the ranks of major competitors. Those key personnel had either left of their own volition, or been sacked. It is often stated, the major asset of a company is its personnel. This is a truism and the case with the Port Talbot Depot insuperably proves this statement. The personnel had gone for whatever reason then joined other competitors and acquired the major cleaning contracts at the Steelworks which at that time amounted to in excess of eighty percent of the depot's business. Richard was given the task of securing new business and reviving the business prospects of the ailing depot, but only allocated a short time in which to do it. Dave Pearce was looking for a way to get rid of Richard by making life as difficult as possible for him. In this day, it is known as constructive dismissal. Of course, as suspected, the task of rejuvenating the ailing depot proved to be unattainable.

Steve Houghton was given a made up position within Hyperwaste after the eventual closure of the facility at Swansea and being made redundant. Upon being made redundant, Steve Houghton was immediately on the phone to Dave Pearce. He had what he wanted, a foot in the door. A leopard does not change his spots and after being employed by Hyperwaste, Steve was constantly on the phone to Dave Pearce, giving him *'feedback'* on all the good work he had been doing for the company, informing Dave of everything he was doing and I do mean everything.

Richard, meanwhile, still had the title of UK Manager Waste Division, but still with the task of trying to increase business for the Port Talbot site for the Industrial division. Because he tended to spend more time concentrating on the tribulations of the Port Talbot depot, he thought it prudent to be based from there and not at the new depot. Besides, Steve Houghton was beginning to get on his nerves. He had to deal with him during the project for Techno-chem, but now he wanted less and less to be associated with him.

It became evident that Dave Pearce was giving Richard grief about the lack of progress concerning his new assignment, until eventually Richard reached the end of his tether, deciding enough was enough and handing in his notice. He left to work for a big company in disposal and industrial cleaning and a major competitor for Hyperwaste. He had taken enough from Dave Pearce. Richard had given everything for the company but now found himself subjected to continual chastisement about his lack of progress. Upon hearing the news, about Richard terminating his employment with the company, it came as no surprise. Everyone who knew him was sad to see him leave, including myself. He had given everything for the company and in the end treated shabbily.

Everything appeared to be going to plan for Dave Pearce and Steve Houghton. Steve was given the job of Area Manager for the waste division. In reality, he knew nothing of the waste industry. Just as he was a nuisance to Richard during his final days with Techno-chem, Steve proved to be a nuisance as South West Area Manager, wanting 'feedback' on everything going on from myself to the depot managers and became known as Steve 'feedback' Houghton.

During my time working for Repeat Control Corporation, we used the expression,' One oh shit is equivalent to one thousand attaboys,' which means no matter how much good work one does for a company, it only takes one mistake to eradicate all past efforts.

Steve Houghton's 'one oh shit!' came in the form of the giant oil company Texaco. Hyperwaste had won a contract for the removal and disposal of approximately 3000 tonnes of organic toxic sludge. Steve decided to take complete control of the project. But being the type of person not to seek or listen to advice, would not listen to people who had worked in the industry for years. He insisted on being informed about everything going on with 'feedback' but often reluctant to listen to any advice. He decided the sludge could be put into roll on roll off 20 tonne skips and then taken to a hazardous landfill site. Karl Barclay had told him the waste should be shipped in tankers and taken to treatment plants for Steve was good at discovering what was going on but not good at doing.

The organic sludge was put into the skips and shipped to the landfill site for disposal. A number of problems arose. Because the material was so wet and mobile, dirty water leaked out of the skips during their journey to the landfill site, the skips are only used for shipping dry wastes. When the vehicles arrived at the treatment site, they were turned away because of this problem. It was at the time, legislation was passed prohibiting landfill sites from accepting liquid waste and the landfill sites ensure they did not break the law for fear of being made an example of as a test case.

The skips were sent back to the oil refinery at Pembroke. It became necessary to hire more skips to hold the waste while Steve decided on the next course of action. Advice was given by the staff and ignored. Meanwhile there were now approximately 100 skips at the site on hire for £2 per week per skip. It was costing Hyperwaste £200 per week just for the skips. This went on for over a month so we are now talking of four figure costs.

Steve was advised to try and dry the waste. Which he did by adding tonnes of sand to the waste sludge which was no good as sand is not absorbent, plus it increased the weight quite considerably. The material was emptied out then mixed in a concrete pit using a JCB.... yet more costs, which once again, proved to be useless.

Steve insisted on phoning Dave Pearce at least three times a day from his first day with the company with it becoming a ritual. Unfortunately, the oil company was not at all pleased with the way the project was going and complained to the Hyperwaste Managing Director. Gradually Dave Pearce began deliberately distancing himself from his protégé, and suddenly started becoming unavailable to take phone calls from Steve Houghton, the same scenario concerning Gerald Charters with the land reclamation project. It became blatantly obvious to everyone, everyone except Steve, that is, his days with the company were numbered. Weeks went by before he held a face to face conversation with Dave Pearce and when he did, it was his last with Dave handing him his P45, with Dave, yet again, performing one of his infamous hatchet jobs.

The main regret I have about the whole Steve Houghton incident is the fact that a really professional, committed, decent guy, I am of course referring to Richard Cooper, was replaced by someone totally incompetent and sycophantic. I believe the company was the main loser in the end.

CHAPTER 20

*W*hile working at the treatment plant, I became friendly with a number of the drivers from the other depots, particularly those based in the South Wales area. A large number of the drivers from those locations tended to avail themselves of the amenities at the treatment plant, particularly the huge clarifier which had been filled with water to hydraulically test the integrity of the huge process vessel. Throughout the summer of 1991, which unfortunately turned out to be the last spent working at the treatment plant, the weather tended to be particularly hot and humid, on some days broaching on being almost scorching. As a consequence, the drivers decided to use the huge settlement tank containing almost 2 million tonnes of hydrant water as their own, purpose-built, company swimming pool, packing their swimming trunks with their gear before commencing work in the morning and changing into their costumes upon arriving at the plant before diving into the freezing water to cool off. The drivers often used the pretext of some minor mechanical problem with their vehicle in order to drive to the plant and get the problem fixed by the diesel fitters. Of course, their ultimate objective in driving to the facility was to indulge in pleasurable aquatic past times and swimming around in the huge clarifier like huge seals.

There were certainly some characters amongst them, such as Derek whose main hobby was racing pigeons, and who talked incessantly about nothing else. Another was Alf Waters, who despite being in his early sixties, married and a grandfather of twelve, appeared to be continually indulging in extra marital affairs, and somehow managing to keep quite a few women on the go at the same time. The reader must take into consideration this was in the days of pre-viagra, so you have to admire his libido and sexual staying power, which most of us did through envious eyes. Almost two years later, on a summer's evening at the new depot near Cardiff, while the fitter's worked late on a vehicle frantically preparing it for plating or MOT the next day, Jacob, one of the mechanics noticed the cab of a Scania in the compound shaking quite violently, as if some mini-earthquake was taking place in its vicinity. Upon approaching the cab to investigate further, he caught sight of Alf indulging in some highly vigorous, energetic love-making with one of his many girlfriends, his posterior going up and down at a great rate of knots while his female companion had her legs clasped tightly around his body. Jacob did not think the libidinous drive or his female lover noticed him, if they did, they carried on regardless, as both approached their climactic peak, oblivious to everything else in the final throes of passion.

Shortly afterward, they emerged from the cab of the lorry, highly flushed after their pleasurable exertion. The three mechanics stood by the doors of the garage and watched as Alf gallantly helped his buxom, middle aged, female lover out of the vehicle. They all the stood and applauded as both lovers emerged. Alf and his female companion appeared quite shameless, in fact once they reached firm ground after descending from the cab, he bowed and she curtsied. Both mature lovers headed imperturbably towards Alf's jalopy, an aged Ford Escort, and drove away.

There was Tommy Morgan who had some disgusting habits, like always wearing the same filthy vest the window of his cab always covered in solidified phlegm where he had been continually spitting out of his cab.

Finally, there was Leonard, who loved relating fantastic humorous stories and which I must confess I thoroughly enjoyed listening to. Leonard tended to be extremely amusing and reminded me of the irrepressible Ronnie Corbet, the miniscule comedian who indulged in monologues during the two Ronnie's show of the eighties. Ronnie Corbett would begin with one subject and then be diverted to three or four other stories before reverting back to the original story or joke. Leonard was exactly the same in his story telling technique, beginning with one story and then digressing to other stories along the way, before finally returning to the main topic of his discussion. One particular day at the treatment plant I watched from the warm confines of the laboratory while Jamie became embroiled in a conversation with Leonard. Weather wise, the day was horrendous, with torrential rain precipitating almost horizontally because of the accompanying high winds. Leonard was safely ensconced within the confines of his warm cab with its diesel engine running, the heaters on high and the blowers going full blast, while he indulged himself in one of his monologues. Jamie stood outside the vehicle looking up at Leonard as he related his story, which, as usual, became quite protracted and drawn out. Despite wearing his wet weather gear, Jamie gradually became soaked to the skin as the rain permeated into any open nooks or crannies in his wet weather clothing, before eventually running in rivulets down his substantial torso. I could see him shivering while he obligingly listened to Leonard as he monotonously droned on. Jamie stood for well over 45 minutes at the same spot before the driver finally ended his story. Shortly afterwards, Jamie came into the laboratory, swearing profusely. Telling everyone present, in no uncertain terms, how cold, wet and thoroughly miserable he was.

'That Leonard, I'm sure he must breath through his arse, it's the only way he can talk so much without appearing to take a breath. It's taken me nearly a fucking hour to finally interrupt him and tell him I had to go. I'm bloody soaked to the skin and fucking freezing!'

Leonard was hard to dislike and loved telling his stories and I enjoyed listening to him. I recall asking him one day if he had always been a tanker driver.

'No,' he replied in his distinctly nonchalant sort of way, before adding in his own inimitable style. 'I used to have my own bakery delivery business before I joined Hyperwaste.'

'What happened?' I enquired, thoroughly intrigued by the statement Leonard had just made.

'I went bankrupt,' he replied, in an unfazed sort of way.

I continued pressing Leonard about the circumstances regarding the financial debacle of his former bakery business. 'Well Vinnie, some of my bread round tended to be in a few deprived, poor areas and as a consequence, quite a number of the women couldn't afford to pay me except "*in kind.*" They offered certain shall we say "sexual services" as payment and with my looks, I have to take it when it's on offer. So there I was with a fantastic sex life, but no real viable income. As well as the financial implications. I had to give it up for my health, in case my wife ever found out and decided to separate my old boy from my testicles.'

I could see his point about taking opportunities whenever they presented themselves, for Leonard was not particularly handsome with a thin, rodent like face. He was 5ft 6in stature, with a body bordering on

218

emaciated, possessing no muscular attributes whatsoever. A prospective Chippendale, he most certainly was not.

He also told me how he often collected the septic tank waste from Tom Jones' huge house which at that time was in the outskirts of Cowbridge. It seemed every time he went there, Linda, Tom's wife offered him a cup of tea and biscuits. He said she was very nice and allegedly enjoyed having a chat with him and she always gave him a generous £20 tip for emptying the tank. No wonder he enjoyed going there.

I loved listening to the stories Leonard often told, a few concerning a local Leisure centre where he once worked as a barman. One of which was totally incredulous. It appeared the local rugby club had a sponsor, in the form of a local builder. In order to advertise his business during the local home fixtures he had a balloon filled with helium which flew above the ground and which advertised his building venture, with the name of his company emblazoned in large letters on the side of the blimp, sufficiently large for all to see.

Unfortunately, the advertising balloon was susceptible to the vagaries of the weather, particularly high winds and prone to break away from its mooring ropes which were there to ensure the balloon stayed attached to *terra firma.* After each break away by the balloon, in order to retrieve it, the builder supplied his men with air rifles which they then used to liberally perforate the skin of the itinerant inflatable enabling the expensive gas to escape. Once peppered with holes, the skin of the balloon drifted in the wind before dropping down and getting caught in tall trees, miles away from the rugby ground. Once retrieved, the balloon required intensive patching due to the accuracy of the sharpshooters. Their accuracy at hitting the balloon, improved considerably as time went by due to the

219

amount of intensive on the job practice acquired over the months. The builder discovered this method of retrieving the nomadic balloon, expensive, together with rifles, pellets, repairs to the skin of the balloon but the highest cost he incurred was mainly because of the helium required to re-inflate the vessel. Helium does not come cheaply and is an extremely expensive noble, inert gas. So each time the balloon required inflating, the costs were immense. Even if the balloon had not been deflated by the sharpshooters, it required deflating at the end of each match still incurring costs with the expensive helium.

The manager of the local leisure centre at which Leonard worked part-time in order to pay off his debts from his loss-making baker round, was a very good friend of the builder. The latter asked if it would be possible to store the balloon at the leisure centre, keeping it tethered and moored close to the ground. The manager agreed and even suggested his caretaker could un-tether the balloon and walk it to the leisure centre located about a mile away casually holding the mooring rope. What he had failed to take into account was the balloon was normally winched down by machinery and when held, it usually took three or four men to stop the balloon rising into the ionosphere. The caretaker refused point blank to walk the balloon from the rugby ground to the leisure centre, knowing full well he would be taken up into the air, his toes firstly gently walking along the ground like a ballet dancer before raising then gliding into the air with the balloon and rising like Felix Baumgartner, to God knows what height.

Leonard also told me a story about the leisure centre when he worked one evening behind the bar. That particular night, it was a ladies evening with a group of male strippers arranged. The women, mostly middle aged, were well oiled having consumed quite a considerable amount of high alcohol drinks throughout the evening. Finally the male strippers appeared on stage to perform their routine. Some of the women, because of the alcohol ingested, lost all inhibition and decided to become part of the show. The performance degenerated from a strip show to live sex acts, with the sexually frustrated, intoxicated women participating of their own volition. The manager decided things had gone far enough and went on stage to put an end to the proceedings. Unfortunately, the inebriated female audience had no wish for the erotic show to end, dragging the manager off the stage before he could put a stop to the evening's unplanned events. It quickly became evident he had a full scale riot on his hands with, the audience insisting the impromptu sex show continuing and he was forced to allow the show to run its full course.

The drivers had their own absolutely wonderful, work place sense of humour. One driver named Dai Jones and who frequently visited the treatment plant based at the Llanelli depot and known to everyone as Dai Version because of his propensity for getting lost during most of his journeys invariably arriving late to wherever he tended to be travelling. The other drivers often referred to him by his nickname, even to his face. Dai always took it with his, nonchalant easy-going manner and accommodating sense of humour.

The drivers always caused Ryan some consternation with their antics and things they did. One driver, Stan had to drive a 40-foot taut liner on a collection. After completing the job, he returned the unit back to the local company from which it had been hired as instructed. Stan obligingly did as he was told and after completing the job returned the trailer unit back to the hire company. Unfortunately, Stan had failed to notice the unit turned out to be just a couple of feet higher than normal sized taut liners and although capable of going under most bridges, a bridge on one of the many roads leading to the hire company, just happened to be slightly lower than normal with highly visible headroom warnings on it. Normal high sided vehicles could just about go under the standard height bridges, however the unit which Stan towed exceeded the low headroom of one particular this bridge on one of the routes leading back to the hire company. Stan took the vehicle under the Bridge at high speed, unaware the trailer would not go safely under the viaduct. Suddenly there was a sickening 'crunch' as the top of the unit hit the underside of the brickwork. Unable to stop in time the vehicle ploughed under the bridge. The metal stanchions on the vehicle took the brunt of the impact, lifting the front of the trailer unit in the process, before the nuts and bolts gave way, pulling them out of the base of the trailer. The other stanchions behind did exactly the same thing as each connected with the bridge, also with the nuts and bolts being pulled out, until the whole curtain edifice, including the roof of the of the taut liner collapsed in a heap onto the base. Stan heard the noise and felt the juddering before, putting on the brakes and coming to a halt, but by that time it was too late and all the damage had been done. He emerged from his cab, afraid of what he would see. It turned out to be far worse than expected. All the tarpaulin, stanchions and top of the taut liner had collapsed like a carelessly discarded pack of cards onto the bed of the vehicle. The front of the flatbed curved upwards, having been peeled back by the impact when the stanchions connected with the low bridge. The front of the trailer bed now resembled the front of a Royal Navy aircraft carrier which had been modified, curving upwards to allow Harrier jump jets to take off, conserving their fuel. Stan looked at the damage to the hired trailer unit in disbelief. Had he been responsible for that? He did not know what to do and instead of reporting the incident to Ryan, he took the trailer unit back to the hire company, parked it on the back lot immediately driving away without informing anyone about the incident.

The next morning, Ryan answered the phone only to be on the receiving end of a torrent of abuse from the manager of the hire company who informed him the trailer unit was just a mass of matchsticks which had been parked in his compound. Ryan had to go and report to him, and eat humble pie. Stan later received his dressing down from Ryan and a written warning.

Some months later, Stan was delivering a load of 205 litre drums filled with resin from my former employer, Cox and Sons. The drums were double stacked on the flatbed. Stan stood on one side while the fork lift driver loaded the pallets from the other side. He misjudged the forks, knocking one of the pallets quite heavily, causing one of the heavy drums to topple over. Unfortunately, Stan was talking to someone and failed to notice the drum as it tumbled menacingly through the air the edge of the drum connected with Stan's foot and in the process almost completely severing all of his toes from his foot. An ambulance was called and Stan was taken to Bedford Hospital, where a surgical operation was performed. Stan lost all of the toes on his left foot and necessitated a few weeks being spent at the Hospital. Gangrene kept setting in and the surgeons had to keep shaving back more and more of his foot. After a month, the doctors had managed to stop the infection spreading and felt confident enough to send him home. Rather than pay for the hire of an ambulance for the journey from Bedford to his home town of Senghenydd near

Caerphilly in South Wales, I was asked if I could collect him on the weekend in my company car. I readily agreed, finding Stan a likeable individual. After Collecting Cynthia, his wife, early one Sunday morning, I embarked on the long car journey to Bedford. Cynthia was good company, quite chatty and helped shorten the journey considerably with her enthusiastic conversation.

During the homeward bound journey, I almost passed out as Stan began describing a minute by minute account of his accident, informing me he was conscious as the porters pushed him in a wheelchair through the corridors of the hospital, trying to get him to the operating theatre as quickly as possible. All the while, being conscious, he could see the five toes of his left foot precariously hanging off the end of his foot, the link being maintained by thin amounts of skin and tissues, with blood everywhere. Trying to get away from the gory details, I asked Stan if the fact he had been wearing trainers instead of Protective work shoes would be a problem for compensation.

'Not at all, in fact the HSE, said if I had been wearing my "*toe tecters*," it would have been worse with my whole foot being squashed under the metal end cap of the shoe and I could have lost my whole foot and it would have been difficult to get the metal protection off.' After what Stan had said, I often thought is it wise to wear proactive shoes in that case. Following Stan's lurid, vivid description of his ordeal, I stopped the vehicle car at the first services to prevent the possibility of me fainting while driving. I used the pretext of having a coffee and a chance to rest a while for the 'pit stop.'

Upon reaching South Wales, I had been given instructions to drop Stan off at Cardiff Royal Infirmary, where he was to continue his convalescence. He underwent a few more operations to prevent the spread of gangrene which periodically re-appeared on his injured foot. Stan never worked again for the company, but did receive a fairly substantial compensation for the accident, primarily from the disposal outlet's insurance company. I don't think he was too upset about losing his job. Stan was in his late fifties and nearing retirement. The fairly hefty insurance payment allowed him to retire without any financial worries in his later life.

I visited Stan on a couple of occasions during his time at the infirmary when he appeared seemed in good spirits following eventual stoppages of the gangrene outbreaks. Cynthia was happy as well. No longer would her husband be away on overnight stays while working as a driver for Hyperwaste. They could enjoy his enforced retirement together.

Finally there was Callum. He could in no way be described as the sharpest knife in the box, although listening to him talking. He had served Queen and country in the army prior to working for Hyperwaste. Jacob unflatteringly remarked if there was another major conflict, Callum's main duty would be as fodder for the cannons.

Ryan Rhys had just received a new company car. He had been driving around in it for about a week with the vehicle eventually running low on fuel and asked Callum if he would fill it up for him. Callum obliged and drove the vehicle to the diesel pump on site and immediately began putting the diesel into the tank of the car. The fitters looked on with glee, and malice as Callum let the diesel flow into the tank. When it was about half full, Jacob shouted over to him, 'You do realize that car is petrol not diesel?'

Callum carried on for a short while, considering the men to be winding him up, but then thought perhaps he

225

had better check, only to discover they were indeed telling the truth. He uttered a few expletives, waiting a considerable amount of time to generate courage before eventually informing Ryan concerning his faux pas. In his defence it must be stated that up until that time all the company cars which Ryan had were propelled by diesel. Although he should have checked before he began filling the tank He had a bollocking from Ryan who called him every derogatory name under the sun. Of course the fuel tank of the new car had to be then drained flushed and thoroughly cleaned before being then filled with petrol, putting it out of use for a few days. Yes, there certainly was an eclectic mix of drivers working for Hyperwaste.

CHAPTER 21

*F*ollowing the dismantling of the Treatment plant, a few years went by, with my base of operations transferred to the depot on the outskirts of Cardiff. For those few years at the new depot time passed by so quickly, seemingly to go by as months rather than years, mainly because my tasks and duties transpired to be so varied and interesting, the difference in my responsibilities making the time go so quickly, allowing me no time in which to become bored. As Albert Einstein postulated, 'time is relative.'

After almost three years following the closure of the treatment plant, Hyperwaste eventually acquired another Oil water treatment facility in Gwent. Ever since the original plant had been compulsory purchased by the Council and vacated in January 1992, the company had constantly been on the lookout for another facility. During 1995, one such plant became available, located in Gwent, South Wales near to the coast. I first became aware of the impending acquisition at the beginning of 1995. During one of his frequent visits to the new Depot, Dave Pearce called me into one of the offices and informed me of the possible acquisition of the existing site.

The proposed site possessed an unbelievably lenient, site licence, permitting unusually high volumes of discharge and consent limits. The consent limits for the effluent discharge had high allowances for oil content, as well as suspended solids and heavy metals content. Far more moderate and lenient than the strict limits, previously imposed on the former treatment site. I had no complaints with these lenient limits making

227

my job that much easier. He also told me Hyperwaste intended buying the site, or to be more precise, paying off the outstanding debts of the company as the payment for the plant. Dave then imparted the name of the owner, which unfortunately turned out to be non-other than Sir Andrew Chadrock Hulsey.

As previously mentioned, I had come across this particular Baronet during my time at West Mercian Oil, also during my time as member of the local Round Table whilst married to Cindy. It was the same Andrew, or to be more precise, the 9th Baronet of Shirebrook from whom I had purchased the Triumph Spitfire Mark IV, the sports car possessing a defective clutch. He was the sort of person who, after shaking hands with, it was advisable to count the fingers on one's hand, just in case he had stolen one of the digits, specifically ones with any jewellery expensive or otherwise attached to them. He would sell his grandmother if a profit were in the offing. The fact he had incurred insurmountable debts, and which and found unable to pay off came as no surprise. It was the way in which Sir Andrew ambled and conned his way through life. It was not the fact Andrew tended to be completely inept as an executive, whilst living a profligate life which grated upon people, but mainly his arrogant, opinionated upper-class attitude possessing no respect for other people, whom he invariably looked down on with disdain, considering individuals existed for abuse and manipulation describing normal individuals as 'plebs.' He also had no respect for rules regulations and laws, considering himself above such mundane things, as I was to discover during my tenure at the newly acquired site.

The deal on offer, apart from paying off all his outstanding debts also entailed giving the Baronet a contract for three years working for the Sales department and receiving a regular salary. The salary on offer was exorbitant when compared with the salary the other sales people received within the company. I questioned Dave Pearce about this state of affairs and the wisdom of employing the unequivocally dodgy aristocrat. Dave informed me if the company did not agree to employ him with an exorbitant salary, he could possibly sell to one of Hyperwaste's competitors. In any case, the company would much rather Andrew 'be on the inside of the tent pissing out, than on the outside pissing in.'

He also told me, following the completion of the sale, the company wanted me to be based at the treatment facility in Gwent and relocate, once again move all the laboratory equipment currently located at the new depot as soon as possible. The negotiations between the company and the Baronet dragged on for months until extreme financial pressure from Andrew's creditors forced him to agree and expedite the sale. During this period, the delay instigated political decisions within UPA, the French company and the predominant shareholder of the company. UPA also owned another waste disposal company functioning within the UK, a company concerned with actual waste treatment, rather than transportation side of the business, specifically incineration of clinical waste from hospitals, laboratories etc. Moreover, they were in the process of setting up an incineration facility in Wrexham, trading under the name of Ortran.

As Hyperwaste looked like successfully purchasing the treatment plant, it was considered perhaps the plant should come under the auspices of the treatment and Waste disposal division rather than the Waste Transport and Chemical cleaning division. Therefore, Ortran should begin having a massive input into the development of the new oil treatment plant. I now discovered myself for a short time reporting to the directors of two companies, the term 'complicated situation' understating the facts, as there was no love lost between the directors of the two companies, apparently with quite acrimonious arguments taking place in the foyers of hotels whenever the two groups of directors met. I had to tread a very wary line and not speak out of turn against either camp or heaven help me. My diplomatic skills coming to the fore.

For the time being, following the acquisition of the treatment plant, I remained at the Depot until the new offices and laboratory became established. The old office which Sir Andrew Chadrock Hulsey worked was deemed unfit as a working environment, infested with vermin, primarily rats, including the Baronet himself.

Nathan Edwards, as the Technical Director for Ortran, was put in charge of setting up the site and getting it operational as fast as possible. He was a Civil Engineer by profession, fully conversant with building laws and the tricks of the trade, particularly when applying for planning consent, and the setting up of treatment plants. He also knew the legislation relating to the treatment of hazardous waste, also how to deal with local Councils. He had immense diplomatic skills which he used to great effect. I saw him charm the young woman in charge of the Local Council Waste Disposal Authority section, prior to it becoming part of the Environment agency. When we all met for the first time, she was extremely reserved and wary, having previously dealt with our tricky knight of the realm. By the end of the meeting, she was eating out of Nathan's hand as he cajoled and charmed her. At the time he was in his mid to late-fifties, average height and slightly overweight, possessing the obligatory middle age paunch. He possessed a mop of thick white hair below which appeared a youngish face exuding an almost cherubic-like smile, rose–red cheeks, adorned with thick glasses. He looked like your favourite uncle, softly spoken but possessing an intellect and perspicacity as sharp as a surgeon's scalpel.

At boardroom level over in France, things came to a head, the major shareholder deciding to amalgamate Ortran and Hyperwaste into one, giving the newly formed company the same name as theirs, UPA, with only one Managing Director required. Both Tom Driscoll and Marcel Aymé disliked each other intensely. Tom told the main French company there was absolutely no way he could work for Marcel and would resign if Marcel became the Chief Executive Officer. I thought his ultimatum ill-advised, with Marcel Aymé, being such a close acquaintance of the French company's Chairman. In addition, he was French and spoke excellent English.

The foreseen transpired, Marcel became Chief Executive Officer of the new company, and Tom Driscoll immediately resigned. The remainder of the Hyperwaste board kept their jobs for a short time. However because most of them had been acolytes and cohorts of Tom, they too eventually went after being called into the Marcel's office and sacked one by one, including Dave Pearce, '*he who lives by the sword, and all that.*' As previously mentioned Dave had always treated me fairly and decently and I felt a modicum of sadness at his departure. There were a considerable amount of people past and present associated with the Hyperwaste who had no such feelings, glad to see him depart in such a humiliating manner. Roger Tate became the head or Managing Director of the transport division of the new company, basically, the old Hyperwaste set up. He had managed to survive quite a few of the purges and now he was in charge of it.

Hyperwaste had more intrigue and plotting than a Shakespearean Play.

CHAPTER 22

*P*rior to the company signing all legal paperwork for the acquisition of the Sir Andrew's facility, I had been instructed to take samples of all the waste oils stored on the premises, as there could be a distinct possibility some of those oils contained small amounts of PCB. Besides having no business acumen whatsoever, Sir Andrew could also be deemed technically incompetent. How a Baronet became involved in the waste industry is beyond my comprehension and understanding, a fact I still cannot grasp some twenty years on. I would have thought with his privileged, aristocratic upbringing and a distinct predisposition towards nefarious, seedy and duplicitous activities he would have been more inclined to a career in politics, investment banking, journalism or something of a similar ilk.

Although initially discovered in the nineteenth century, PCB (Polychlorinated Bi Phenyls. Not to be confused with Printed Circuit Boards) were only produced in vast quantities from the late nineteen twenties onwards, mostly by the giant multinational conglomerate, Monsanto. Initially the new wonder chemical was primarily used in transformers as an alternative to the flammable mineral oils being used at the time. Later, PCB also had other uses as plasticizers in the paint and polymer industries. When fully developed and mass produced, PCB fulfilled the requirements and everything demanded of transformer oils, ticking all of the boxes listed below:

Non-Flammable.

Extremely good electrical insulation properties.

High boiling point.

Viscosity and characteristics of medium grade mineral oil.

High Viscosity Index (the viscosity varying little with large temperature changes).

Good heat transfer properties, primarily for the cooling of transformers.

Chemically stable not breaking down over time and immune from oxidation.

Thus when PCB eventually became available in vast quantities from the late1920's onwards, Electrical Engineers thought this new transformer oil a wonderful phenomenon. However, as the decades evolved it became evident the newly developed, chemical had a downside. Being so chemically stable PCB could not easily be broken down. When combined with standard mineral oil in low concentrations and the mixture burnt, highly toxic chemicals called dioxins become formed and then generated in the gaseous emissions due to incomplete combustion, making the mixing of PCB with fuel oils an environmentally harmful proposition. The only way in which PCB can be broken down safely without any adverse effects to the environment is by specialised high temperature incineration i.e. burning at temperatures in excess of 1200 degrees Celsius. During the eighties and nineties, only two incineration facilities existed in the United Kingdom possessing the technical capability for the safe disposal of large quantities of the toxic transformer oil. Unfortunately, using this state of the art technology for disposal of PCB came at a prohibitively high financial cost.

Land filling of PCB also became illegal, with the product not breaking down naturally, having the potential of still being around in thousands of years' time, leaving an unwanted legacy for future generations. The chemical also has the capability of being able to dissolve extremely slightly in water and the possibility of seeping into water courses.

The final downfall and ultimate demise of this wonder oil came as a result of its suspected links with cancer and its cumulative accrual in the breast milk of lactating mothers, in addition to its build up in the eco-system such as soils, and water courses in the realms of parts per billion. Before the twentieth century, nowhere in nature did PCB exist. Today, in the new millennium, PCB's are everywhere and an inherent part of the environment, wholly generated by humans.

Because of all the medical findings, in the seventies and eighties, the use of PCB in transformer oils became banned worldwide. However, the complete eradication of PCB, which still exists to this day in large amounts, is on-going, with thousands of ancient transformers still in use all around the globe which still contain the highly toxic 'transformer oil' awaiting disposal by the only feasible environmentally safe method, high temperature incineration.

Sir Andrew possessed no proper, expensive analytical equipment for determining whether any of the oils which he took onto his site contained PCB, and he certainly would not pay for outside costly analysis by independent laboratories. If any of the oils on his premises happened to be contaminated with PCB, they could only be disposed of by means of high temperature incineration as mentioned, incurring the subsequently exorbitant, and hefty disposal costs. As a final safeguard, it became my task to take samples of all the oil storage tanks, sludge, soil and water to determine whether any PCB contamination actually existed on the proposed acquisition. The last thing Hyperwaste wanted was to take over the premises and discover they had been burdened with a gigantic bill for disposal, after purchasing a PCB contaminated site.

235

Everybody was aware Andrew would most certainly not be forthcoming with any information concerning PCB contamination if he was indeed cognizant of the fact.

Weeks prior to the decision to go ahead and purchase the site, as instructed, I took large amounts of samples of the oils, executing an extensive sampling regime, meticulously logging the areas from which they had been taken, and numbering the samples, then performing analysis using the Gas Liquid Chromatography, as well as some analysis carried out by an independent laboratory to help spread the workload and an additional safety check. This work went on for weeks, with Karl Barclay assisting. Fortunately for the company and I suspect more by luck than judgement on the part of our Baronet, no PCB manifested itself on the site.

It was during this time I first became acquainted with Andrew's workforce based at the treatment plant. Though why anyone would willingly choose to work for Andrew was beyond me. After talking to them, it became apparent Andrew took every opportunity to short change them of their rightful earnings whenever the opportunity presented itself.

My workload appeared to be increasing exponentially and the Directors observed I was being stretched and pulled in all directions. Finally they decided I needed an assistant. After conducting numerous interviews, the company eventually employed Paul, a young Industrial Chemist who had been made redundant from British Steel. Having Paul on board doing the analysis and helping in the laboratory helped reduce a considerable amount of the workload from myself, ameliorating the pressure.

Both Tom Driscoll and Dave Pearce had, by this time, ceased to be employed by the company, Tom having jumped ship and Dave in his turn, pushed, that is to say, sacked.

Roger Tate became elevated to the position of Chief Executive Officer for the existing Hyperwaste division, which now became part of UPA. The treatment plant became part of the Ortran division and Marcel Aymé became head of the newly formed, merged company. Nathan Edwards became his second in command and given the responsibility of getting the new plant up and running and profitable. I initially had a limited amount of dealings with Nathan prior to the acquisition, however, as time went on with the final purchase of the site nearing completion, my contact with Nathan became more frequent, finding myself reporting to him on a regular basis.

Following months of negotiation, legal searches, investigations, completion of the sampling regime and the conclusive evidence of PCB absence, the plant was finally acquired. During the last weeks prior to Hyperwaste taking over, I visited the plant to determine where the new laboratory would be sited. Nathan Edwards had already drawn up site plans for a weighbridge, location for the new laboratory and the filter press from the old site which had been held in storage since the closure of the facility.

While on site, I talked more frequently to Andrew's workforce. On the following Monday after the final agreement and acquisition had been signed, they would become part of the UPA payroll. Until that moment, they technically still worked for Andrew. However, that last weekend, he had asked them if they would agree to work on one last chemical cleaning job for him somewhere in Slough which meant an overnight stay for the Saturday night with the job anticipated to take all of Saturday and most of Sunday. The guys asked me if it was alright for them to carry out work for Andrew during that weekend. I informed them, they did not actually become part of the UPA payroll until the following Monday, so it was entirely up to them if they wished to earn some extra cash by working for their former boss, although I strongly advised against it as they had no workers protection with his company which technically no longer existed, but stipulated they must be available for work with UPA on the Monday morning.

They actually carried out the work for their old employer, but he never paid them the full amount promised for their labour and their time spent away from home. Later, during his frequent, unwanted visits to the plant, Andrew always managed to fob off his former employees whenever they approached him about the outstanding remuneration which he owed them. He had no need of them now, with them working for the UPA and consequently believed he had no need to pay them what they were morally owed. It was during this time, despite his boyish appearance, I observed what he was really like, duplicitous, sleazy, and arrogant and an extremely tricky entity to the last.

The first Monday, Karl Barclay went to the plant after been given the job of Site foreman. I was still based at the depot, awaiting the demolition of the old office building, previously home to numerous rats including the former owner. All the laboratory equipment could not be moved until the aforementioned had been completed and a new portacabin put in situ. The first morning of the changeover, I received a frantic phone call from Nathan Edwards, almost verging on panic stricken.

'Vinson, get down to the new site at once, the boys have phoned me to say they think there is something wrong with the diesel contained in the storage tank.'

238

'What's the problem?' I asked trying to calm him down, for Nathan had a tendency to lose control of his English stiff upper lip when highly stressed.

'They wouldn't say, just they believe there is a problem with the diesel which they are using in the vehicles.'

Immediately, I collected up a number of glass sample bottles and drove to the newly acquired site, leaving Paul to look after the laboratory and deal with any technical questions from the other depots.

Arriving at the site, I enquired about the problem concerning the diesel. The new workforce advised me to take a look for myself. After sampling the diesel tank, it became evident the fuel was a homogeneous mixture of red and white diesel, which I guessed to be approximately a fifty, fifty mix of the two types. Our Baronet had been running his on-road vehicles using red diesel, a totally illegal practice, depriving the Inland Revenue of extra taxes. Immediately phoning Nathan, I informed him of the situation, knowing full well the reaction I would get, hoping he would not take it out on the messenger and shoot him, i.e. namely me.

After being brought up to date concerning the situation, all I could hear coming down the line from Nathan was a huge list of expletives spoken in an extremely refined, well-educated English accent. The swearing appearing quite incongruous and out of place with the well pronounced enunciation and English accent Nathan possessed.

'The fucking bastard!! What a fucking twat, I just knew he couldn't be trusted!' Nathan realised he should have instructed me to take samples of the diesel prior to acquisition and an oversight on his part. After eventually climbing down from the ceiling, metaphorically-speaking, Nathan regained his composure and began issuing assertive instructions.

239

'Vinson, tell the guys to drive the vehicles down to the Depot and order them to take it easy and not drive too fast. The last thing I want is for one of them to have an accident or get stopped by the police. I'll phone the depot and tell them to flush out all the vehicles' fuel tanks immediately. God, I hope they don't get stopped, otherwise all the vehicles we have throughout the country will be taken off the road. It could mean financial ruin and scandal for the company. Technically, all of his vehicles now belong to us!'

Upon questioning the wisdom of his decision, enquiring if he considered it sensible to drive the vehicles to the depot, Nathan insisted he wanted the vehicles to be flushed at the depot where the company had the proper facilities for carrying out a thorough and complete decontamination of the vehicles.

Gratefully, one by one, the entire fleet, previously owned by the fraudulent Baronet, managed to be successfully driven to the depot and the illegal fuel eradicated from their fuel tanks without any mishaps. After talking to the plant's workforce, it became apparent the vehicles had been running on red diesel for well over a year. They knew it was illegal and had often made their boss aware of the facts. He, of course, chose to ignore their protestations, carrying on regardless. The situation had now altered and they did not want their new employer to face litigation and the possibility of becoming unemployed themselves.

Months, prior to the final take over, Nathan had drawn up plans for the site. The week of the acquisition, he began putting his ideas into operation. Karl, my old mate and I had both been instructed to use the newly acquired site as our base. Paul Macdonald performed my duties at the depot, issuing the Technical Advice Documents (TAD) and doing any chemical analysis required. If he encountered any problems he contacted me. I was also told emphatically, any projects for other company depots were to be ignored and to be carried out by external Chemists. My primary duties now lay with getting the newly acquired treatment plant operational and instigating any changes required.

Firstly we had to go through the old site office and sort out the paperwork and any important documentation prior to dismantling and removing it from site. During this time we came upon Andrew's HGV Class 1 licence. Andrew had often bragged to all and sundry how he possessed a HGV class 1 and able to drive his articulated tanker on customers' premises, particularly during high pressure jetting operations. Gerald, one of his men was a qualified tanker driver and he always drove the tanker to the sites, but Andrew often drove the tanker around the site. The licence we discovered in the desk only turned out to be a provisional licence and not a full licence. I do not think Andrew's customers would have been too happy had they known an unqualified HGV1 driver had been driving an articulated vehicle around on their premises. It appears to us mere 'plebs,' the aristocracy are inculcated with a belief they are superior, in the scheme of things and above the laws of the land.

For the next few weeks, following the purchase of the site, Andrew kept turning up unannounced continually interfering, giving his unwanted opinions. In the end the situation became intolerable. I phoned Nathan who had a word with the baronet and told the former owner to butt out and stay away and only use the transport depot as his base of operations.

Other situations materialized because of Sir Andrew's double dealings. The sales department of Hyperwaste took on a new salesman, Lawrence, who was also based at the Bedwas depot. Years earlier, Lawrence had owned his own waste oil business and an old acquaintance of the Baronet. Sir Andrew had sold him a high pressure jetter / tanker for around £40,000. As expected, when dealing with Andrew, the tanker turned out to be a complete load of rubbish and broke down within a few days of the purchase, requiring extensive, prohibitively costly repairs. Lawrence complained vociferously to Andrew that he had been 'sold a pup' and wanted all of his money back. Andrew refused, despite numerous solicitors' letters and threatened court cases. Lawrence never retrieved his money and after some months of expensive legal wrangling, went bankrupt. Whenever the two of them met at the depot, the pair would end up arguing violently, almost coming to blows, requiring some nearby neutral parties wrenching both protagonists apart.

Hyperwaste had dealings with a disposal outlet located on the outskirts of Port Talbot. One of the directors who ran the company had, at one time been employed by Hyperwaste. While talking to him one day, it came to light, he too had been involved in financial litigation with the Baronet. Previously, Dave, the director in question had once been a business partner of Andrew's. As with a lot of relationships, it fell apart. Dave had wanted to sell his share of the business back to Andrew rather than continue with the acrimonious partnership. So it was agreed the partnership would be terminated. Unfortunately, Andrew was not forthcoming with the agreed amount of £60,000 and refused to pay. Yet another, long drawn out court case ensued, the outcome of which deemed Andrew should pay Dave the £60,000 immediately and also pay the court costs, another example of the Baronet's arrogant, dismissive attitude towards other people.

Things began to move swiftly on the new site and the old offices dismantled and disposed of. A building contractor was hired by Nathan Edwards. The contractor's first job was to completely concrete the area where the original office had been located, then concrete the whole grounds outside the bunded tank areas and to excavate a section for the new weighbridge to be located at the front of the pre-fabricated office and proposed laboratory block.

During frequent discussions with Nathan concerning the state of the existing storage tanks, we agreed, most of the storage tanks on site had seen better days and in need of replacing. Nathan asked what type of tanks would be best suited. I advised him to get vertical tanks with heating coils, to speed up the oil water separation process and easy access through manholes top and bottom for maintenance and cleaning.

The plant quite quickly began taking on the appearance of a building site, with concrete being laid, replacing the black hardcore. An area was quickly laid and the new office located onto it. Once that had been done, I had the task of getting all the laboratory equipment, removed from the depot and installed. Thankfully, Paul was there to help me with all of that. Having twice previously installing the equipment, it was all done relatively quickly. And we had our new office block and laboratory in situ within a couple of months, minus any of the original domicile rodents.

The weighbridge was then installed in front of the new office block. Oils from the antiquated existing tanks emptied and sold as fuel oil, then the tanks, cleaned, dismantled and sold as scrap. Nathan was in his element looking for replacement tanks, adhering to the agreed specification. He appeared to have the ability to by stuff on the cheap. I have not seen him for many years since those heady days, but I can imagine him spending most of his twilight years in the new millennium trawling the internet on web sites such as eBay and Gum Tree looking for cheap bargains on offer.

There was a lot of chemical engineering involved with arrangements, pump specifications according to the requirements, Arranging for the location of the old filter press from the former treatment plant, and the attendant powerful reciprocating Willett pumps. So much welding and pipe laying was required, two fabricating contractors were called for. Once again, I was having a fabulous time, Paul took care of the laboratory and the paperwork side, and I became involved with setting up the plant and dealing with the contractors in Nathan's absence, with instructions to give him a full update at the end of each day.

Forecasts had been made about the amount of soluble oil, acids and alkalis expected to be received on site. Andrew had not been involved in that side of the oil treatment, just reselling mineral oils. It was decided a huge tank would be required in which to store the incoming water based oils prior to treatment. BSC Whiteheads Newport was closing and selling equipment, one of which fortuitously managed to be a huge vertical storage tank.

Following negotiations with the managers at BSC Whiteheads, it was agreed we could have the huge oil storage tank capable of holding (40,000 gallons). When Nathan and I informed the MD of one of the contractors of our intentions, he replied he would like the contract for the dismantling, having a friend who owned a haulage company with low loaders specialising in moving large equipment and tanks. We took him and the haulage contractor to the tank at BSC. After carrying out some measurements they both exuded an aura of extreme confidence which indicated they would be able to transport the huge tank the three miles through the busy streets and thoroughfares of Newport without any difficulty whatsoever.

The next few weeks, Ryan Rhys arranged for some of his men to clean out the huge tank, ensuring any residual heavy fuel oil left inside was removed. The next stage was for the MD of the fabricating company and his men to either cut or uncouple the pipe-work connecting the tank to the main site, cutting sufficient pipe work, allowing the tank to be transported through the town safely.

Finally the day arrived for shipping the huge tank from BSC Whiteheads to the newly acquired treatment site. All the necessary people were informed - Council, Police, Highways Department and the time and date for removal set, mid-morning on a Friday. Nathan came down to visit the site that day but left the logistics and details to the contractor and his haulage friend.

That morning, Nathan and I were en route to the depot for a pre-arranged meeting, when Paul Macdonald phoned, informing us the low loader vehicle shipping the huge container was stuck outside the Royal Gwent Hospital. It appeared not enough of the connecting pipe work of the tank had been cut away allowing it to pass easily through a set lights for a pedestrian pelican crossing. The contractor had miscalculated in his mental arithmetic resulting in the low loader becoming stuck on the main road unable to move through the two uprights of the pelican crossing. Furthermore, the traffic had built up behind the vehicle inhibiting its ability to reverse backwards. Gridlock in the Newport traffic system now ensued, with all movement of traffic gradually grinding to a halt. I thought I was about to have a heart attack and considered heading towards all the chaos in the town and began manoeuvring the car. Nathan suddenly grabbed hold of my arm.

'What are you doing?' he enquired.

'Don't you think we should go and assist?' I replied, my throat croaking due to the apprehension and dryness being experienced.

For once, it was Nathan who remained calm and not the other way around. 'The contractors have arranged all this. They are the people acting on our behalf. They said they could do it and it is up to them to sort it out. We just stay out of the way in the background and let them get on with it,' he replied calmly.

I gazed at him incredulously. To be honest, Nathan tended to be a bit of a control freak, usually insisting on taking charge of most situations and events. I fully expected him to go dashing in like John Wayne and the seventh cavalry in an attempt to save the day. However, in this instance he was more than happy to stay on the sidelines allowing the proceedings take their course. Being his subordinate, I acquiesced to his instructions and continued driving to the transport depot where we had a pre-arranged meeting to attend.

Somehow, after much disruption to the Newport traffic system, the two contractors, the fabricating company and the transport company, managed to get the huge tank back to the original BSC site from where it had come and the tank off-loaded from the vehicle. That afternoon, the welding team set to work cutting off the protuberances on the tank, this time cutting right to the circumference of the tank, ensuring no repeat of that day's events.

Following all the mayhem caused that Friday, the police would in no way countenance transporting the tank on a busy normal, working day insisting instead the tank be moved early Sunday morning. So it was arranged to ship the tank 8:00 the following Sunday.

Despite Nathan's objection, I insisted on being at hand during the operation. Because the MD of the welding company and his haulage friend had made a mess of the move, we incurred no additional costs, with the re-run being done at their expense.

The Sunday morning arrived, after I had experienced a torrid Saturday night, finding myself unable to sleep, concerned as I was about the second attempt at moving the huge storage tank. I went straight to the site at BSC. The heavy crane was in position and the tank put back onto the low loader making certain the tank was centrally located on the vehicle. Mercifully, the transfer went like clockwork and the tank managed to be negotiated successfully through the two uprights of the pelican crossing. Men walked ahead of the slow moving vehicle, with huge poles possessing 'u' shaped prongs on the end to elevate any low cables hanging across the urban roads of Newport. The final difficult section occurred on the industrial site where the treatment plant was located and where there happened to be a very low bridge. I had negotiated with the managers of another BSC plant, obtaining their permission to take the huge vessel through their facility and out through the back gates. This operation meant altering their one way system during the move. It being a Sunday morning, this caused no major problems. Finally, the tank arrived at the treatment plant where the second crane waited to off-load the tank onto the concrete plinth which had been laid weeks earlier. The whole operation was finally completed by 10:00 am that morning. I was so relieved everything had gone like clockwork, phoning Nathan to inform him of the good news. While talking to him, I distinctly sensed the relief in his voice and demeanour.

After dismantling most of the original plant, the ten or more second hand replacement tanks which Nathan had ordered began arriving. These tanks were uniform in size, at about 25 feet tall and 10 feet diameter and for transportation, strapped to the beds of ordinary 40 feet articulated, flat bed vehicles. Because of the low bridge on the industrial site, all the vehicles had to travel through the steelworks similar to the huge storage tank. All had to be arranged with the management of the nearby steelworks. Times of arrival had to be co-ordinated with the site security for them to divert the traffic on the site. This plan ran like clockwork until one day. For some unfathomable reason, the last vehicle carrying a tank, piggy backed on the flatbed travelled to the plant without any one being aware of the fact. Subsequently the vehicle arrived at the works site and because they had not been informed of its arrival and need to go through the works, the security department refused access.... there was probably a '*jobsworth*' in charge that particular day.

After waiting on site for a considerable period of time and ultimately being refused access, the driver became disgruntled and decided to try his luck taking the tank via the low bridge route. Unfortunately, his gamble did not pay off and the vehicle became tightly wedged under the structure. Fortunately, although the bridge was low, the road tended to be quite wide and other vehicles using the access road were able to negotiate around the jammed vehicle. Nathan Edwards phoned informing me about the incident and that was my first knowledge. I drove around to find the rather large driver standing forlornly outside the cab of his vehicle, puffing heavily on a cigarette. He had managed to get the tank half way under the bridge, but now it was firmly stuck.

I looked at the vehicle and asked the driver if the trailer unit would drop much if the cab unit were removed. He told me it would drop approximately a foot. But then asked 'Why, what are you thinking of doing?'

An idea came into my head, if we could drop the trailer unit slightly, it may then be possible to pull it through. I explained my reasoning to the driver. 'But how are you going to pull it, the front unit needs to be coupled to pull it and the front legs of the trailer will drag on the tarmac, they are as low down as they will go.'

We had a crane on site for moving equipment around and told him I intended to use it to lift and pull the trailer with the tank under the bridge and hopefully through to the other side. He looked and then said 'It won't work, you are out of your mind!'

I drove back to the treatment plant and told the crane driver to take his vehicle to the bridge. I also press ganged some of the workforce and contractors. When the crane finally arrived at the scene, the front lorry cab was disconnected from the trailer unit and the legs of the unit were wound down as far as they would go, the tank was now just below the girders of the bridge and not touching it. The hook of the crane had ropes tied around it and the other end of the rope looped under the base of the unit and passed behind the front legs of the trailer and then knotted.

Once everything was in place, the crane lifted the front of the unit, sufficient enough to take the bases of the legs off the tarmac. However in lifting the trailer unit, the tank again came into contact with the girders of the bridge, again becoming slightly jammed. One of the contractors suggested the idea of letting down the tyres, which did not please the driver. I thought why not, it's worth a try? We let quite a bit of air out of all the tyres, and tried again. Lo and behold, much to my relief, it worked. The trailer unit dropped which then dropped the perimeter of the tank away from the girders allowing it to move freely. The unit and tank were then gingerly pulled under the bridge by the crane. Fortunately on the treatment plant we had a small compressor for putting air into vehicle tyres. The lorry cab was re-coupled to the trailer unit an then driven slowly to the site without any further mishaps. From then on all high loads had to obtain permission before setting out and a time agreed with the access site.

Throughout those early days, more evidence of Andrew's numerous dishonest, duplicitous activities began coming to light. Often Karl went to the local suppliers with some of Chadrock Hulsey's workforce to buy consumables such as PVC gloves, hosepipes tape etc. However, as soon as the suppliers were cognizant of the fact we had taken over the site, they refused to provide the goods before monies upfront. Nothing could be bought with a purchase requisition. Chadrock Hulsey owed money to a large number of suppliers, the total amounting to thousands of pounds and unfortunately, having taken over the facility, Hyperwaste now became tarred with the same brush, by association. This payment up front caused horrendous problems as we did not carry large amounts of petty cash at the site. One by one, Karl managed to persuade the suppliers to provide equipment using purchase requisitions, which made life a lot easier. I could not believe the amount of money Chadrock Hulsey owed to the local business community and nobody had a good word to say about him. Hyperwaste had only paid off his major creditors such as the banks, he had neglected the small suppliers and left them to take the losses.

Even Lady Cynthia possessed the same arrogant tendencies. The story goes, one Christmas period she visited the plant. Andrew had stocked up with some alcoholic beverages which his wife began consuming in copious amounts. After sometime she decided to drive home, despite her obvious intoxicated state and being incapable of driving. Sure enough, she had hardly left the gates of the plant before running her expensive BMW into one of the street lights, completely mangling the front of the car, also badly damaging the street light in the process. Staggering back to the plant, she tearfully explained the situation to her husband who then instructed his workforce to get the fork truck and tow the irreparable car back onto the site before the incident was reported and the police became involved and Lady Cynthia being prosecuted for driving a vehicle while under the influence.

The Baronet even managed to trick Ryan Rhys, who up until that time I had considered to be the master of the shady deal and con artist extraordinaire. During the acquisition of Sir Andrew's companies by Hyperwaste there were numerous pieces of equipment purchased. One of which was an expensive piece of high pressure jetting equipment, which through lack of maintenance and repair could not be used. Sir Andrew had managed to put in a tender for a chemical cleaning job with large company near Reading. He persuaded Ryan to pay out almost a thousand pounds to service the equipment stating they would need it for the contract. Ryan did as requested and paid for the equipment refurbishment.

The company did not get the contract. But soon after the equipment had been serviced, it unexpectedly vanished, never to be seen again. The rumour was Andrew had been involved in some way and after persuading Ryan to get the equipment serviced, managed to get it out of the area and sell it on quite easily. The suspicions were never proved. However, everyone who knew Sir Andrew believed he had hand in it somewhere along the line.

A number of storage containers began arriving on site containing all the old equipment from the previous treatment site and which had been put into storage. Nathan had arranged for the whole site to be concreted, and the black existing hardcore completely covered. The only problem was the storage containers were in the way. The solution was to get them off the site for the time being while the concrete was being laid, but not move them a large distance.

Karl had noticed the premises adjoining the site possessed plenty of empty, unused land. He suggested we should contact the owner and ask him if he would temporarily allow us to store the container units on his land. The adjoining premises recycled waste cooking oils and the recycled product then used in animal feed.

With the hope the owner Ben Rogers would agree to let us put the containers on his land, Karl and I went around. We had to go to the adjoining site on quite a few occasions. For it appeared every time we did so, the owner, Ben was too busy and unable to meet with us. This continued for almost a week, and time was getting desperate, we needed to move the storage containers, as the building contractor wanted to begin putting down the concrete as soon as possible and the containers prevented a start being made. Then one morning I managed to stop Ben while he was driving out through the gate of his premises, persuading him, albeit reluctantly, to hold a meeting later that day with Karl and myself.

True to his word we met at the agreed time in his office. He was blunt and to the point in his comments. 'This is nothing personal against the two of you but, if you are associates of Sir Andrew Chadrock Hulsey, I don't want any dealings with you or that bastard.'

Karl and I just looked at each other, fully understanding his attitude towards Andrew. Informing

Ben we too had 'no truck' with Andrew emphasising he now had nothing to do with the site, having been instructed to keep away by the directors. Karl interjecting saying emphatically 'We don't even like him and try to have as little to do with him as possible, although he does still work for Hyperwaste.' Karl felt personally aggrieved, experiencing great umbrage at being considered a friend and associate of the untrustworthy aristocrat.

After perceiving our genuinely antipathetic attitude towards the former owner of the site, Ben mellowed slightly towards us and began explaining the reason for his animosity towards Andrew. It seemed that Baronet frequently discharged illegal amounts of sludge and oils into the sewage system. When the Regulatory Authorities made enquiries, and pointed the finger at him, Sir Andrew always managed somehow to pass the blame onto Ben, whose plant, unfortunately, discharged into the same effluent system and consequently Ben was forever being pursued by Welsh Water Authority and the NRA, all because of his neighbour. Ben was innocent yet, because of Andrew Chadrock Hulsey, appeared to be continually in trouble with the legislative authorities. Over the years, experiencing numerous such incidents, Ben's dislike of his neighbour gestated into intense detestation and hatred. Ben was another individual our Aristocrat managed to antagonise and alienate, displaying a trait in which he rather excelled.

Whenever Nathan was not around, he relied upon me to ensure the work progressed as quickly as possible, insisting upon a verbal report via phone at the end of each day and often during the day. Nathan's main problem was his verbosity, during our conversations, which could become quite protracted, creating an unwanted diversion to my normal working day. I recall one day he phoned me at about 9:30 in the morning just for a chat about the Civil and mechanical work programmed for the day. My thoughts were '*Oh God, here we go another hour long conversation*!'

He casually remarked about the oils being received on site. Suddenly as if by magic, Robert Jones, one of the local Sales engineers walked into the office. Robert had told me earlier about a large amount of mineral oil requiring disposal from the giant steelworks at Port Talbot, I casually mentioned the fact to Nathan who insisted upon talking to the sales representative. Knowing full well the conversation would go on for some time, I went about my work. An hour or so later, Rob came off the phone after his 'ear fucking' by Nathan. 'He doesn't half go on,' I thought he would never get off the line.' The worn out expression on his face telling of the ordeal he had just been subjected to.

Half an hour later Nathan phoned back, remembering he had wanted to talk to me. He asked how the concrete laying was progressing, when the main civil engineering contractor walked in. Once again I passed the phone out to the wing. 'Funny you should say that,' I said to him, 'Peter, the Civil Engineer, has just walked in.... he can update you himself.' With that I passed the phone to Peter, carrying on with my paperwork. Once again the conversation lasted over an hour. and once again I was given another haggard look, this time by Peter ' I wouldn't like too many of those conversations!' he remarked and vacating the office as quickly as possible just in case Nathan decided to immediately phone back.

Later the Director did phone back to continue with our interrupted conversation. After a quick word he remarked, 'How is the pipe work and welding progressing?' With that, the Managing Director of the fabricating company walked in and once again, I passed

254

Nathan over to another unsuspecting businessman, with yet another hour long conversation taking place.

The same procedure took place, after the MD also had his 'ear bashing'. He ran out of the office as fast as possible. Unfortunately, fobbing off my boss backfired, as later that day he phoned me back at around 5:30 that evening. 'Yes you little bastard!' he remarked somewhat jokingly. 'You've managed to fob me off all day, I want to talk to you about the plant!' With that, he kept me on the phone until 7:00. I guess during his working life, Nathan must have spent over half his working day on the phone.

Another evening, he left the Newport site to head back to his home in Chester, enlightening me about some old friends visiting him and his wife that evening, with the intention of staying for the weekend and he wanted to be away from the site by 4:30 at the latest.

Nathan, being the type of person he was, phoned me on his hands free at 5:30 during his homeward journey to ask some questions, despite having been with me all day. Suddenly, in mid-sentence, I heard a chilling 'Aaaaaaaaaargh,' immediately after which, the line went dead. I rang back at once, only to get the unobtainable message on his mobile, phoning his mobile quite a few times, only to get the same response. Then, I phoned Ryan at the depot, in case he had the phone number for Nathan's home, which he did not. I also contacted other directors to inform them about what had just transpired. About three quarters of an hour later, Nathan phoned back. He sounded shaken, his voice quivering as he talked.

It appeared during our conversation, while driving towards the brow of a hill on the outskirts of Hereford, a car travelling in the opposite direction was turning right into a side road from the main road immediately crossing in front of his car, just as broached the brow.

255

Unable to take evasive action, he ploughed straight into the car. He informed me he was okay and uninjured as was the female driver of the other car. His mobile phone was damaged and he had borrowed a bystander's phone to contact me. He gave me some numbers to contact, especially his wife, informing them of the accident. That incident brought home to me the dangers of talking on the phone while driving, even on hands free. A new hire car had to be brought to Nathan in Hereford and he eventually arrived home at 2:00 am the following morning. Despite his accident, Nathan still continued to use his mobile, albeit hands free while driving. I liked Nathan but as my mother used to remark, 'He could talk the hind legs off a donkey.'

Gradually and inexorably, the plant began taking shape, with Nathan always on the lookout for more business, insisting on taking in oils which were viscous and far too difficult to process, causing problems for myself and the operators. My workload had increased hugely. Thank God I had Paul to assist me and take some of the burden. Since the days of Dave Pearce, I had not received an increase in pay for some time since his generous increase and a few years had elapsed since then.

I had tremendous respect for Nathan Edwards both as a boss and as an individual. However, when it came to awarding pay increases, he could be as tight as a duck's arse and one would have thought it came out of his own salary, the way he performed about it. Every time I brought up the subject concerning my low pay, he would come up with some excuse or other, such as stating the plant, being in its early days was at that time not making a profit with no extra money in the coffers to increase my pay, even suggesting that in a year or two, I could be on a bonus and part of a profit sharing scheme, benefiting when the old treatment plant started going into the black. I felt hard done by, having worked tirelessly for the company and yet they persistently avoided giving me a pay increase, forever dangling the carrot in front of me. Throughout the years, I had put in many extra hours with no additional overtime payments or recompense.

This time, I decided to shuffle my deck of cards and not wait for fate to manipulate my life. After perusing through the 'careers section' of the papers, one particular job jumped out from the page for which I appeared eminently suited with a hazardous waste incineration company. The remuneration was almost thirty per cent more than my current salary with generous overtime payments a company car, so I would not be losing out in that respect, also with my own expense account. After re-arranging the cards of life, I waited to see the new hand dealt me and which direction my life would take.

What a journey that eventually would turn out to be, with all sorts of ramifications and consequences, resulting in another marriage and a complete career change, working for a department known as 'Special Operations.'

But those are stories for another time.